It's Not all Rainbows and Ponies

A Memoir

Laura Shepperd

ISBN: 978-0-9973885-0-3
ISBN: 0-9973885-0-1

Acknowledgements

Thanks to Sharon Kuhn Young for her enthusiasm, encouragement and expertise, without whom this book would still be sitting on my computer. To Cheryl Brown, for hours upon hours of honest criticism and daily encouragement. You are my person. To Angela Huffhines and Sandra Shirey for reading and editing multiple drafts, and for cheering me on.

The people and events in my story are true. Names and details regarding individuals have been changed for anonymity.

Those I spent that summer with are forever my trusted friends, and our bond is strong. I hold them close in my heart and continue to pray for their health and happiness.

For Andy, Dale, Jennifer and Sarah

*It's Not All Rainbows
and Ponies*

The first drink. It was the only one I ever really wanted,
but never the only one I had.

Chapter 1

"Are you going to drink tonight, Mom?" Alli asked.

"I don't know," I shrugged. I was sitting on my bed with stacks of clothes for packing. I couldn't bear to look at her, so I kept folding, stacking and re-stacking my clothes. I didn't know what the hell else to do.

"Not drinking would be a good start," she continued. "It would show something. It would be *something*."

"Yeah, it would be. But I don't know." I didn't want to make one more promise I couldn't keep, and God knows I could use a drink. I was going to Rehab in three days, and that's all I knew about anything. I'd made the call, suffered three brutally honest telephone interviews, confirmed arrangements, and announced my plan to my husband when he got home from work. Yep, I did it all on my own – drunk on my ass. Now I was living in some surreal state of limbo, like that awkward time after a death in the family when all the arrangements have been made, and everyone wanders around aimlessly, eyes glazed over, waiting for someone to say, 'Go.'

Leroy told Alli about my decision. She had just graduated from college and was back home to get some money in the bank as she started her first teaching job. Our oldest and his new bride were settling into their new home and jobs several hundred miles away. Our youngest was away in his second year of college. Mom's going to rehab. How embarrassing for them. If I allowed myself to think about it too long, the shame would fill me so that I was sure something would crack to relieve the pressure. I might throw up, or worse, start a cry I feared might never end. My solution? Autopilot.

Those last days at home I stayed in my room, mostly. Intellectually, I knew there was much to do before checking out of life and into Rehab, but emotionally and physically, I just wanted to lie down. Just lie there in hopes that others would execute my latest plan to make things better. Reservation made. Load me up and ship me off. It was paralyzing. I did manage a trip to Wal-Mart, but I wandered up and down the aisles for more than two hours and came home with some travel-sized toiletries and a journal. Leroy appeared to be on autopilot too, and I was good with it. What else *could* he do?

Alli hardly spoke to me in those awkward days before I left. There really wasn't much to say anyway, I'd told myself. I was pretty sure she was mad at me. I knew she was disgusted with me. My heart ached that our relationship might be damaged for good, but now there was nothing I could do but push through until I made it to Rehab. I never doubted for one second that she was behind my decision, but she had to work through it in her own way. She was one strong chick, and I knew she would come out on the other side. She was my Alli. The day before I left, she found it within herself to be helpful, and even make some loving gestures.

"You'll need some pictures," she said in a matter-of-fact

2

tone. "I'll get some from my phone and computer and print them off for you."

"Perfect." I gave her a weak smile. I had thought of it. I had thought of a lot of things, but I couldn't move on any of them. I could try to pack, but that was all I could do.

"Will we be able to talk to you?" she asked later. She was sitting on my bed, trimming up photographs.

"Oh, I already got that cleared up during all these phone calls," I said. "I told them I won't do well without talking to my kids and my husband. I told them I need my family. I mean, I would get depressed otherwise, and that can't be helpful."

"And?" she asked, looking exasperated.

"They said absolutely we could talk. I was so relieved."

"Makes sense." She nodded and continued working on the photos.

"I mean, I just don't do well without my family," I said. "That just wouldn't work for me. It would make things worse, and I just can't bear ..."

"I know, Mom. It's true. Family is it."

"It *is* it. It's everything." My voice trailed off, as I refolded and re-stacked. I didn't know if she was cutting me off because of my languishing over my family after betraying them for the interloper alcohol was too little too late, or if talking about family was just too painful. It could have been because I was rambling on and on like an idiot. I didn't ask. I didn't feel I had the right to ask.

Alli tossed the stack of pictures on the bed and left the room. I sat on the side of my bed and stared at my bare feet, flat on

3

the hardwood floor. *I did it. I slammed on the brakes. It's over. This is the end, and I don't even know what comes next. I'm completely empty. I hope Alli can find it in herself to still love me. Wonder if she'll always look disappointed when she sees me ... and what a disappointment I must be to my boys. My God, how embarrassing for them all!*

I spent a lot of time on my summer break in that room, making to-do lists that would only end up serving as coasters for the next drink. I tried so very hard every day to be positive when I woke. I would start with the best of intentions in the morning. I set goals for the day, every day. There was plenty of clearing out and re-arranging to do after all three kids moved out – not to mention the last few years of drunken neglect by me.

I'd like to tell you that our three kids leaving for college back-to-back and my eventual empty nest was the cause of my drinking. I'd really like to tell you that's why I couldn't get off my ass and clean daily stuff up and old crap out, that their leaving was just too much for me to bear. But, while it probably intensified my drinking, the truth of the matter is, I couldn't process it. My alcoholic body and mind had me so self-absorbed and emotionally crippled, when it came time for them to leave the nest, I had very little of the real me left to cope. The real me. Taught my daughter to value her person, not her beautiful appearance. Taught my boys respect and discipline. Pushed each one as needed while cheering for them all the way. Called them on their bullshit. Laughed with them all – a lot. Loved them every day and told them so. My heart and my mind knew their leaving for college meant I'd done some

4

things right. "Give 'em roots and wings," my mama would say.

I had been floating through the days of my life for several years, and now I was circling the drain. Everything about me was circular, my drinking, my thinking and my plan-making and procrastinating. I would consult my list from the day before. Nothing marked off. I would either add to it or make a nice fresh handwritten copy.

But then I just wanted one little grapefruit and vodka before I got busy. *What's one gonna hurt? I'm on break, after all.* That first drink always tasted so good. It was really the only one I ever wanted, but it was never the only one I had. I would prepare it with much care, and then sit, sip and mull over my list for the day. In those last days, the Drunk Thinking would start as early as the very first drink.

There's a constant internal dialogue of both arrogance and self-loathing inside every alcoholic and addict, but when drinking or using, both the volume and the intensity are magnified. My drunk thinking was a distorted, fucked-up weave of righteous indignation that unraveled in a heap of self-loathing thread that was then woven and unraveled over and over again. It's a terrifying cycle, and even more terrifying is the hopelessness of not knowing how to get out.

"I deserve a drink. I've earned it for God's sake! I can't believe anyone would question that after all I've done." Then the unraveling. "What's happening to me, and why can't I stop it?" I know it sounds crazy, and trust me, it is.

Externally, good was never good enough, and where I was,

never where I wanted to be. If a task had been accomplished or a good time came to a close, my perpetually restless response was a demanding, "Now what?" Nothing good ever comes in the Drunk Thinking.

Poor Leroy would come home to God-knows-what. He never knew how he would find me, and I'm sure the anticipation and dread made it hard to come home at all. I might be "napping." I might have driven over to a friend's house seeking companionship and confirmation of my perceived profundity. In that case, I would turn off my phone and begin formulating excuses and lies to be told whenever I happened to wobble into the house. He finally quit trying to call me.

As unbelievable as this may seem, this shit sneaked up on me every day that last summer. It was as if it had never happened before. I really thought I could have one drink on any given morning, no problem. Each day was a chance to start anew, right? Yet I was doing the same thing every single day, and I was totally baffled at the result—every time.

One day that summer, not long before I called Rehab, I'd had so much to drink that I passed out by mid-morning. I gasped myself awake, sitting up straight, rigid, my head back, emerging from the deep end of the vodka pool, not knowing the day or the time. Panicked, I sat up in bed. My eyes shot to the windows. It wasn't particularly bright or dark. I quickly slid off the bed, ran down the hallway and into the living room, my heavy feet pounding the hardwood floors in our old house. I stopped cold in the middle of the room, as framed pictures of our kids vibrated on their tabletops, the aftershock of my drunken plodding.

"Where is Leroy?" I whispered to myself. "Leroy!" I screamed. My heart was pounding. My mind was racing. *Where could he be? Why would he leave me? Where would he have gone?*

"Leroy!" I screamed again, rushing through the dining room towards the kitchen. My grandmother's china rattled in its cabinet, and our two Labradors startled and stared as I stomped through the rooms. I jerked open the back door and checked the carport. My car was there, but Leroy's truck was gone. I quickly walked back into our bedroom and checked the clock on the night stand. I whispered the time to myself, as if it were some clue in a larger mystery. I had no bearings—when I fell asleep, what time I woke up, how long before my husband would be home, if my husband would be home. I was gripped with fear.

"Leroy!" I shouted again.

Now the dogs were up, following me in my search. Each time I shouted his name, they would cock their heads in confusion, whimper at me and then look around the room frantically. I checked the clock again. My breathing returned to near normal, and my heart slowed a bit as I realized it was four-thirty in the afternoon, and Leroy was at work.

What the hell is happening to me? Why in the world am I so confused? How could I have slept that hard? Something is very wrong! And then, the inevitable. *Whew! That was weird. I'm gonna need a drink!*

My first year as a school employee with a summer break,

and it was going to kill me. I was going to drink myself to death, knew it, and couldn't even stop it. It was as if I were watching my own tragic demise from outside myself. I never told anyone of that terrifying day, or even allowed the memory of it before Rehab. It would bubble up occasionally, but I was a pro at smashing the hurtful, embarrassing and otherwise uncomfortable back down into a deep, cavernous place I'd created inside of me. I would later come to know that's where shame grows.

*   *   *

Alli had come a long way to get to the point of lovingly preparing sentimentals for my time away. Just days earlier, I'd overheard her grilling her dad about my choice of treatment centers. "Why does she have to go so far? I mean, it's going to take an entire day just to get her there, and then when she's gone, she'll be so far away! Do we even know if we can visit her while she's there? While she's *way* the hell down there?"

"This is where she wants to go, Alli, so this is where she's going," he had answered quietly, but I heard him anyway.

Such was our household in the days between my resolve to go to Treatment and the actual day I left. I was talked about in other rooms as if I weren't home. I could hear the gist of the one-sided telephone conversations and could have filled in the rest, but I chose not to. It was all a moot point, anyway. Things were bad. I was really bad. I was going to Rehab. Any whispers or inexplicable eye contact between Alli and her dad were really of no concern to me. I was going to Rehab, for God's sake! What else could possibly be of any significance at this point? What else could anyone say that would make it better or worse? I had disconnected.

I did have phone calls to make, and I was intentionally putting them off until the night before I left. I wanted to be able to say for sure when I was leaving and when I was expected to check in. Those would be the only things I could know for sure. Once I'd made the call to Rehab, most everything forward was out of my hands as long as I stuck with my decision. The plan was laid; I could repeat it, short and sweet. Repeat it times two for my boys, times four for my siblings and to my mother. *Jesus Christ, that's a lot.*

No one could tell me when I would get out. The counselor on the phone estimated forty-five to sixty days based on my drinking history. *My Drinking History. Humiliating.* It scared me to think about being gone–checked out of my life–for that long. I didn't even know if I would be allowed to leave Rehab if I changed my mind, and I didn't ask for fear of the answer. It really didn't matter to me. For whatever reason, I had made the call, and this ship was sailing.

Chapter 2

"I thought I had more time! Oh my God!" I was crying and pacing back and forth in our bedroom.

"Slow down. Explain to me again what they said." Leroy was trying to be the voice of reason.

"I could be in there as much as forty-five to sixty days. But ... I mean ... even if I bust ass and get better ... I mean, if I'm really doing good ... thirty. I asked them if they thought I could work really hard and get out sooner, but they ... the lady I was talking to ... she said, she said that wasn't likely to happen." I kept running my hand through my hair, front to back, over and over and over. I knew it was manic and weird, but I couldn't stop. "I'm going to run out of time! Our summer break is over sooner than I thought!" I was screaming, crying, and pacing. Leroy was dumbfounded.

"I've got to call Jon. This is terrible! I wanted to take care of this over summer break, get better, get back, you know? I've just screwed this whole thing up. I mean, I've got to go ... but I just ...."

"Slow down, Laura. I'll call him. Then I'll call you," Leroy said.

I was Jon's secretary at the high school in our small country town, and we had just finished our first school year working together. He and his wife had been our friends for more than eight years. I was muddying it all up, asking for personal favors affecting work. Worse, I was asking my husband to call his friend – my boss – for personal favors affecting my work. I muddied up a lot of relationships.

"I hate you doing this as his friend when it's work, and *I* work for him, you don't. And I hate, hate, HATE that I'm putting him in this position!" I was hysterical.

"Stop," he said holding both of my hands. "I'll call him. He'll call you."

I went back to my futile cycle of folding and stacking of clothes, pairing outfits then unstacking, refolding and placing them back in drawers. I had some sense of the craziness of it all, but I was manic and couldn't stop myself. I was standing at my closet, wondering what people wear to Rehab when Jon called. "Jon, I'm so sorry to put you in this situation. I really am."

"It's okay. We'll get through this." His tone was that of caring concern. I was expecting strained, awkward, God-knows-what, but not this, and it was a comforting surprise.

"I'm sorry, Jon. I've got to go, but I'm so sorry about all this."

"We'll get through this. It's going to be okay. I knew you had to do something."

He knew I had to do something? What the hell? Well, of course he knew. I imagine most everyone knew I had to do something. We finished up and hung up, and I returned to my stacking and unstacking.

"He said that?" Leroy was peeved, which surprised me

more than anything Jon had said. I assumed they'd been talking about my drinking. I'd been embarrassingly drunk at Jon's house so many times over the past few years; it would be crazy to think they *hadn't* had a conversation about my drinking.

"He knew you had to do something? I can't believe he said that to you!" He was shaking his head in disbelief.

"What's he gonna say, Leroy? It's not like our friends don't know," I said shrugging my shoulders. I was back to rifling through my closet again. "Him saying it out loud doesn't change anything, really."

Most all of our friends were drinkers. It's what we did when we gathered after our kids' sporting events or to watch a big game, especially when we were younger. Some of the wives didn't drink at all, and others would have an occasional glass of wine or a beer. I suppose that's why I always left the women in the kitchen and gathered outside with the men. There was a time when I could drink with the best of them, and I absolutely loved the rowdy debates and laughter that grew in intensity and volume as the night went on.

But those days for me were long gone. I had become a sloppy mess of a drunk. I never intended to get sloppy drunk, or to offend my friends with my boisterous, foul mouth in front of their children, or to be passed out on a lawn chair in the middle of a party – that's not who I am! But then it was. Near the end of my drinking, it happened so frequently I no longer even apologized. I was genuinely remorseful each and every time, but apologies are meant to be followed by change, and mine never were, no matter

12

my sincerity the morning after. My solution? Just don't talk about it.

But now, something had changed. I wasn't angry or bitter at the thought of people talking about my drinking. I wasn't paranoid that they were talking about me, but the thought that they had didn't threaten, anger or surprise me. I went back to staring into my closet.

Chapter 3

There's no denying the magnificent beauty of the Texas Hill Country, even if you're on your way to Rehab, five hundred miles from home. Traveling southwest from the Piney Woods of northeast Texas where we live, the two-lane roads cut a path through dense forest, then rise to hilltops where rolling green pastures dotted with horses and cattle are occasionally interrupted by oil and gas wells or trailer parks that quickly flash out of view as more pine trees either fill the hillsides or block the horizon completely. Further south, the trees first begin to thin out, then they get shorter as the wind picks up through the plains of Central Texas, which soon begin to roll down towards the Texas Hill Country. What the Hill Country is lacking in tall, lush trees, God made up for in beautiful rolling hills, and the roads cutting through create a roller coaster view of limestone cliffs and green valleys, all leading in and out of nowhere, then into important cities like Austin and San Antonio, and then back out again. Harley riders and deer love this countryside, and boats and fish fill the lakes and streams.

Alli drove me down – eight long hours. We talked everything we dared about Rehab. We talked about everything *but* Rehab. We played amateur designers and pieced together Alli's dream apartment after she gets on her feet financially. I received a lecture on how my life and certain friendships would have to change when I returned home. *When I return home. So far and foreign, I can't even think of it.* Alli's college roommate was a nurse who had worked briefly in a substance abuse wing at a hospital. She told Alli I probably would live like a hospital patient when I first arrived. In a right-side-up world, parents talk to each other about these embarrassing concerns for their children. But there was no horror at the thought of Alli telling her friend. No shame.

I had imploded. The world shrunk. I was oblivious to anything external. Once combative and controlling, now diminished to a submissive recipient of fate. I need not question or inquire about the external. I wasn't worthy of an answer anyway.

I pondered what my detox would entail. "Mom, you think you'll have to be detoxed? Really?" Her face showed fear and panic and her voice, disbelief that this shit could get worse.

"Yes. I didn't think about it at first, but yes." I had visions of being strapped down in a white room. I bit my lip, looked out the window and asked, "Do you think they'll be nice to me?" but Alli never answered.

As we traveled further from cities and closer to my new home, the winding roads narrowed, and what had been intermittent rain turned to buckets of water slapping our car and blocking our view. Mud and rain flowed across the blacktop road into the Guadalupe River on our left.

"Really?" I said. "No rain all damn summer, but it's going to rain as I enter Rehab? It's so cliché!" I lit up a cigarette and looked out the window. I wasn't steel with resolve, but I wasn't weepy either. I'd like to say I was gutted up for the battle of my life, but it wasn't like that. I was battered and busted. Defeated. I was leaving my world behind, heading for isolation, and I couldn't find one single morsel of me. The old me—the real me—the one hidden somewhere inside, would have been strong and determined, ready for the race. The drunk me, well, she would've had a drink! But I didn't. I just sat all hollow inside and fidgeting and fretful on the outside. Occasionally, a wave of panic would rush in, and my organs felt like separate living beings, wriggling against each other inside my shell. I would lean over with my head between my knees and mash my fingers against my temples really hard, and an involuntary low, breathy moan would come out of me. Alli finally had enough.

"What is *that*?" she asked.

"I don't know. I don't know. I'm just getting so nervous." I was rocking back and forth.

"Well, we're not doing that anymore. You can do something else."

"Okay. Sorry. Really, I don't know what the hell," I said.

Alli just shook her head and kept concentrating on the road. Later, it struck me as funny because my moaning probably sounded sexual to her. As if this day weren't weird enough, now her mom is making involuntary sexual moaning sounds. Poor girl! But rather than acknowledge that, I nodded in agreement and released a heavy sigh (*sans* moaning). I shifted in my seat and lit yet another cigarette.

We continued down the winding road through the sheets of rain. Top and bottom, everything was gray, with the low clouds above us, and the steam rising up from the road below. The middle–the trees and grass–were a lush green. The Guadalupe rushed along beside us to our left, and a wall of earth to our right closed us in on the narrow road. We could see houses up beyond the wall. Some of them were beautiful large homes, and others were simple weekend bungalows. All of them had beautiful, well-groomed yards, and the grass and trees would have giggled with delight at the rain if they could. Instead, they just pushed all their green to the front, and it was brilliant. I was wondering how close we were when my phone rang.

"Hello?" I covered my other ear to block back the sound of pouring rain. Alli turned off the radio. "Yes, this is Laura." It was someone from Rehab.

"Are you driving?" she asked.

"No, my daughter is driving me down," I answered, looking at Alli with a shrug.

She wanted to know when to expect me and asked where we were. I assured her I would be arriving on time, but she gently corrected me. Between the rain and our current location, there was no way we would be there at my expected three o'clock check-in time. *Crap. Late as usual.*

"Oh, I'm so sorry, but it has been raining on us the last couple of hours."

"No problem at all, Laura. Just be careful, and we will see you when you get here. Are you doing all right?"

17

Am I doing alright? Let's see. My daughter is driving me to Rehab five hundred miles away from home, so no, it's not my best day.

"Yes ma'am. I'm doing just fine." I looked at Alli, and we both shrugged.

"What's the deal?" Alli asked after I hung up.

"Just checking on me and wondering when we'll be there. Weird."

"That's not weird. I think it's nice."

We continued on, mostly in silence. I dug through my purse, counting cigarette packs, lighters, and money. I looked at my lipstick. I pulled out bundles of unpaid bills and threw them in the backseat. I unbuckled my seat belt, turned around and rifled through one of my bags in the backseat.

"What are you looking for, Mom? Thought of something you forgot?"

"No. I don't know. I'm just looking." I turned back around and stared out the window. My stomach felt hollow. "We're really close. We're getting really close."

*   *   *

The guard house at the entrance gate was barely visible through the rain, but I could see its red roof and the yellow and black reflector stripes on the vehicle guard arms, down on either side to stop traffic headed in and out. Alli slowed the car, and I said, "It's a guard shack, and there's a guard in there. Hmmph." We locked eyes for a moment, and she eased up to the gate.

"How y'all doing on this fine rainy day?" An older man

leaned out of the window to greet us with a big smile.

"We're good," Alli said. *Good as it gets in the situation, I guess. How the hell do you think she's doing on this fine rainy day, dropping her mom off in Rehab?*

"Who have we got there with ya?"

"Her name is ..."

"Laura Shepperd," I interrupted. *She shouldn't have to answer that, like I'm so pitiful I can't speak for myself.*

"Well, welcome! Welcome, Laura!" He checked his clipboard, stretched through his little guard shack window out into the rain and extended his hand to me as I leaned across Alli to meet his.

"You are welcome here, Laura S., and thank you, little lady for giving her the ride down!"

Alli and I smiled and laughed awkwardly, but his smile was genuine and his presence, calm and reassuring. He pointed us to the administration building just to the right past the gate.

*   *   *

"Let me take your picture, and then I'll give you two a few minutes," the admitting lady said turning a camera on her computer monitor towards me. *Probably have to wear an ID so orderlies can call me by name when they chase me back into my room.* I imagined this was how someone would feel being locked up against her own will. *All rights revoked, shut the fuck up and climb on in!* I didn't know that, but I didn't ask because I felt unworthy of answers. I'd waved the white flag, after all. She stuffed my paperwork in a folder and came from behind her desk

19

and headed toward the office door. "Do you have a phone?"

I went cold. "Uhh ... I do. I was going to send it home with my daughter ... I mean, if that's okay. Can I call my husband and let him know we're here, please?"

"Sure you can!" she said smiling.

Whew! I had really worked up some bizarre scenarios in my head over the phone and other restrictions I'd read online about my Rehab. No cell phones, computers, iPods, radios or other electronic devices of any kind allowed. Would they back me in a corner, making demands, snatching and grabbing things from me? I had primed myself for anything.

"It's not a problem. Take as long as you need, and I'll give you two a moment for goodbyes as well." She shut the door behind her.

"She seems nice," Alli said. "And this place seems nice."

I felt like a kid on the first day at school. This role reversal was too bizarre. *The lobby and this office are probably showy, clean facades like those motel lobbies with beautiful staircases leading to nowhere. They do this to make our families feel better. They're probably dumping me in a cold, white-tiled basement once Alli is out of sight.*

Alli and I stood as the lady left the room, stared hard at each other for a few seconds, and then practically dove into each other. Neither one of us had cried until that goodbye hug.

"I love you, Alli," I whispered in her ear. "I love you so much. Thank you." Our bodies were shaking, and soft sobs were breaking through our strongest efforts.

"I love you too, Mama. It's good. This is good." She was barely able to speak through her tears, and it broke my heart. My soul honestly hurt that I was putting her through this pain.

"I'll be good, I promise," I said pulling away and flashing a quivering smile. She laughed through tears, and we both knew we had to stop this now if it was ever going to stop. "Please be careful, Alli. You know I wish you would make a stop and not drive all the way back tonight. You could stop and stay with Nana, and ..."

"I know, I know." She was still wiping away tears as she opened the door and stepped into the hallway.

"Everyone okay?" the administrator asked. We gave her a nod, flashed a glance at each other, and then my Alli was gone.

The letting go had begun. I'd let go and admitted I needed help. Now I had to let go and trust that Alli would make it home safely, even without phone calls and texts from me. I had to let go and trust that my family would hold together and lean on each other while I was away. Most of all, I had to let go and trust that these people knew what the hell they were doing, and that they could help me get better.

Farewells and finances squared away, I was moved to medical intake, an exhausting process triggering an internal clash between my arrogance and humility, perceived independence and realized desperation. My denial and the truth. This mental and emotional mayhem so consumed me, the intake process itself assumed the form of a dreamlike stage production with me being thrust into my assigned seat while invisible stage hands shifted the props and people before me with no transition. I had no context for the disjointed scenes or dialogue I found myself in.

Chapter 4

Alli was gone, and I was in a golf cart with a nurse in the pouring rain. She did her best to chat me up with friendly questions about me and my family, but it felt forced and awkward.

"Where are my bags?"

"They will catch up to you. Gotta be searched first." She kept her eyes on the rough road ahead.

"Did you see a small pink gift bag? It's like a lunch sack shape. My daughter gave it to me just before she left so it wasn't inside my bags. Did you see it with my things?"

"I didn't see any of your things, honey. Your bags went with someone else. No need to worry. You'll get your things when they assign your bed."

Assign my bed? What the hell have I done? Will Alli's pink bag pass inspection?

The cart bounced down a large hill, across a creek shaded by live oak trees and into a parking lot at the bottom. A building that looked like the backside of a motel with some kind of glassed-in offices or rooms at the bottom rose up from the parking lot in front of us creating a canyon of sorts with the hill behind us. We turned left in the parking lot towards a smaller tan metal building. With the tall one closer to my right, now, I could see it was a bland cream color, and through the gray of the rain, it looked very institutional and sad. My stomach sank. I looked and listened as best I could through the pounding rain for anything or anyone. Nothing. Not one soul was moving, talking or even wailing in discomfort. There was just rain and sad, sad silence.

I wonder how many people they let in this place. Where is everyone? Probably on some kind of lock down.

"Alrighty, Laura! Don't forget your purse, and we'll just walk right around here to that door on the side," she said pointing to the right side of the metal building. "Don't slip now!"

And out into the rain we went, ducking our heads and hopping around puddles as best we could. The rain fell in sheets, and once it slapped the pavement, it ran quickly downhill towards the creek in both wide paths and trickling little streams. There were little rainbows and dancing water droplets on the pavement. The rain smelled good, and the trees and flowers that had somehow managed to survive the months of drought and one hundred-plus temperatures seemed to smile as they brought forth their green colors for what was surely the first in a long time. Watered plants don't shine like plants watered with rain.

"You'll check in here and then see the doctor," she shouted over the rain pounding the metal roof. The door was on the back corner of the metal building with an alleyway between it and the sad two-story building. It all felt a bit cloak-and-dagger back in that dark corner as buckets of rain fell between the two, and water splashed up on the back of my legs and soaked my sandals before I could get inside.

*   *   *

"How much do you drink a day, Laura?" A nurse was looking at me over the top of her glasses. We were in a stark, small office with a metal desk between us.

What the hell? Are we just throwing this right out here? Rude!

"Uh, well ..." I looked down at my sweaty hands, and then tucked them under my legs. Then I looked at a painting of a creek or a river or something with large, knotted trees on the bank, and ...

"Laura, how much do you drink, Hon?"

"Wha? I'm sorry. Ma'am?"

"How much do you drink a day?"

Hell, I quit counting years ago ... then started counting again, trying to police myself. Yeah, that didn't work too well, even when I ...

"Laura?"

"Oh, sorry. Well, I guess somewhere around eight or ten."

"Okay. Thank you. When is the last time you had a drink?"

I crossed my legs and pretended to be adjusting the strap on my sandal. *It's so freakin' hot in here! But her desk feels cool on my foot. Weird.*

"Laura?"

"Oh. Last night. I drank last night."

"How many drinks did you have last night?"

"Probably seven or eight."

"Were they bar drinks?" she asked, holding her index finger and thumb apart to indicate a cocktail-sized glass, "Or at-home size?" She was holding both index fingers apart to indicate a tumbler-sized glass.

Well, at least there is some improvement on this one. "I had cocktail-sized drinks last night," my index finger and thumb indicating likewise. Then when I saw them trembling, I quickly pressed my hands together and squeezed them between my knees. I realized I was rocking back and forth a little like Rain Man and quickly stopped myself. While she wrote, I mumbled, "But that's certainly not the usual size for me." She shook her head knowingly and kept on writing.

She was a beautiful silver-haired lady who I guessed was in her sixties. She wasn't particularly warm, but definitely not clinical to a cold fault. She asked about my drinking like any other nurse would ask about a cough or stuffy nose.

She needs to know I'm not like some awful drunk. I go to work. I cook dinner. I've been involved with my kids. She doesn't care. I go to Rehab, that's what she knows. Whoa, file this under places I never thought I'd be, doing things I never thought I'd do! What's happening here? I'm shaking inside and out! My body wants to burst out of my skin! I'd asked for this – I'd made the call, after all.

"Okay, now blow." The nurse was holding a little black box in front of me with a white plastic straw sticking out of it.

"What is that?" I asked.

"Oh, you haven't had to do this ... yet?" She looked over her glasses again with a sly grin.

Breathalyzer? Wow. It's not like I'd walk in here drunk.

Good grief! Wait ... I could've had a drink on the way down? Hell, I didn't even know that was an option! Well, I was with Alli, so...

So I blew, and then I took my cup to the bathroom as instructed. My legs shook as I straddled over the toilet. *Don't sit down in here! God only knows what kind of people have been in this bathroom!* My legs were like Jell-O as I wobbled back into the nurse's little office and sat on my side of her desk, which was practically in the doorway. She opened a packet, took out some small plastic squares and started several urine tests right there on the desk in front of me. I pointed to one.

"What is that one?"

"Pregnancy test."

"Well," I scoffed, "if that's positive, you best be right with the Lord, because some serious stuff is about to go down!"

"You never know what we'll find in these tests."

"Well, I'm just saying." *You never know? What exactly does that mean? What could they find? What else would they find?"*

There was a blur of more blunt, non-judgmental questions after that. Any illicit drugs? Any prescription drugs? Do you have any legal issues pending? And again, When did you say was the last time you drank alcohol?

I felt as if I had been stripped naked.

*   *   *

"Push against my hands with the backs of your hands as hard as you can," a lady in a crisp, white coat said. She was standing facing me with her arms held apart, just inside the width of my shoulders on each side. I dutifully raised my heavy arms in front of me and pushed outward against her hands with the backs of my hands.

"You're strong!" she almost shouted with a laugh.

You have no idea. She was a doctor. I checked her tag. She certainly didn't look like one, though. I was sitting on an examination table, fully dressed with my shaky legs dangling off the end. I glanced around as best I could without risking eye contact. The exam room was very large, but otherwise it looked like any other doctor's office with jars full of cotton and counters covered with silver examination tools. I realized I was leaning on my arms, and my hands were gripping the edge of the table so tightly my knuckles were white. I released my grip, shook my hands a bit, then put them under my legs.

"What's your drug of choice?" she asked smiling, looking directly into my eyes.

Drug of choice? "No drugs." I lowered my head and stared at my feet. I started swinging them hoping the shakiness would subside.

"Okay. So you drink?" She was looking at her clipboard.
"Yes."
"How much do you drink a day, Laura?"
"Too-damn much," I answered with a weak smile.

She laughed, and we made real eye contact this time. I liked her smile. She still didn't look much like a doctor, though. She was short and chubby and wore no make-up. Her skin looked like she spent a lot time outdoors. *Probably a hack, as in Couldn't-*

28

Hack-it Anywhere-Else, Hack. Abortion clinics and rehabs. I guess the bottom of the class has to work somewhere.

"And how much is 'Too-damn?'" she gently pressed on.

What the hell with these questions? So abrupt and, well, in my face! Who talks about this? Who just comes out and asks this shit? What difference does it make, I'm here, aren't I? Besides, I'd answered that question with the nurse earlier and at least twice on the phone over the weekend. Clearly, these people need to communicate better. Share your goddamn notes, already!

"What? I'm sorry, Doctor. What were you saying?"

She was standing at the counter now with a pen in one hand and the other in her coat pocket. She was turned toward me waiting for my answer. I didn't want to be as rude as the thoughts in my head were. These people were running the show, for God's sake! I was pretty sure they were going to be running my life.

"I was asking how much you drink a day."

"Oh. Uhm, probably somewhere between ten to fifteen."

I almost paused to qualify it with *You know, depending on how it was at work or if we are with friends,* but I knew damn well it didn't matter. I drank that way every single day. Might as well be honest for once. More questions.

"Cocktails? Wine? Beer?"

"Cocktails." *Surely this is almost over.*

No lecture. No parental you-should-know-better looks. She just smiled and began reviewing her notes. For one brief moment, I wondered if this were all a weird dream that would soon be over, but the next, panic filled me, and I imagined my escape. I would

29

laugh, shake my head, and make some joke about this entire situation being a huge misunderstanding. I would apologize for wasting her time, and tell her to just forget our conversation. I'd made entirely too much out of my little drinking problem. But there it was, in writing, forever. *I just said that out loud, and she just wrote it down. That nurse wrote it down too. There it is, forever. What the hell have I done?*

"Okay. Now, if you'll just lie back for a moment," she said, gently placing a hand on my shoulder and the other on the small of my back.

I laid back, stared at the ceiling and, like at the gynecologist, tried to just go someplace else in my head. She pushed and pressed my gut and up under my rib cage. I wondered if my liver was enlarged, but I was too embarrassed to ask. I remembered standing naked in front of the bathroom mirror at home with my arms raised above my head, checking to see if my liver was sticking out from under my ribcage. Somehow, self-examination of my breasts was too weird, but this particular exercise was not. Go figure.

She finished up with routine exam stuff from reflex checks to a little pen light in my eyes. I thought about my cloudy eyes. I thought about all the drops I'd put in my big brown eyes over the past few years, telling myself it was for allergies. But they weren't just red, they were a hazy yellow, and I knew it. It made me sad. It filled me with shame. Every single day I looked in the mirror, I felt sad and ashamed.

"Okay, Laura. If you'll follow me now," she said. "We've

missed the lab today, so we'll get your blood drawn tomorrow."

I'm not sure what I expected, maybe stern looks and lectures on my behavior, but nothing this clinical. I slid off the examining table, paused to make sure my legs were going to hold, grabbed my purse from the counter and followed her down a hall of seemingly endless twists and turns.

They're going to put me in the hospital. I wonder if they'll strap me down. What if scary, fucked-up people, wandering all around in their fucked-upness are in there with me? There's no telling what kind of people are in this place. I haven't seen them, but they've hidden them somewhere in here. I hope Alli is safe driving home in this rain. I wish she would've stayed in a hotel. She might fall asleep. It's too far for a one-day trip. I should have pressed her harder. My chest feels tight. I hope this lady is a real doctor.

I felt as though my soul had been examined by strangers, but how could this be true? I certainly had been examined physically, but had anyone dug deep into my psyche? There had been no probing questions about my childhood. No interrogation as to the circumstances of my drinking or the consequences suffered. Yet, in verbalizing the truth about it, I felt as if I had been split wide open and examined deeper than tissue, even deeper than bones. Deep places I had long since hidden from myself. Those secret shameful places that had been mine and mine alone, no matter how exhausting it had been keeping them that way. It was at first intrusive, then violating. It was my reckoning.

Chapter 5

The doctor lead me to the admitting room of the Special Care Unit (referred to as the SCU), which looked like a miniature E.R. Small clusters of desks with accompanying visitor chairs created a reception area. There was a glass wall with a door leading outside to my left, facing the parking lot and creek from earlier. There were glassed-in cubicles to my right with desks and visitor chairs. *Probably all glass because they need to be able to see in there in case any of these people go crazy. There's no telling what kind of stuff has gone down in this place!*

Stereotypical cranky-looking old nurse? Check. She was at the front desk. Effeminate male nurse? Check. He was working in one of the glassed-in cubicles. My folder was given to one of the nurses, and I was asked to sit. All alone. No bags, no phone, no family. Just paperwork. Like an orphan.

*   *   *

My God! That old guy looks super drunk!

He looked to be in his late sixties, maybe early seventies. He was wearing khaki shorts and a bright red polo that matched his face. His arms and hands were weathered like my dad's. I wondered if he had worked construction too.

"Howaryu?" he asked leaning toward me in a wobbly fashion, with his hand extended. I thought he might teeter all the way out of his chair. He withdrew his hand, using both to steady himself on his chair.

"I'm fine, thank you," I answered.

"You waitin' to see the nurse guy too?"

He turned around to point towards the male nurse in the glassed-in office behind him. When he turned his head, his whole body followed clumsily. I leaned towards him, not knowing whether I should try to catch him or call someone for help. Once I was sure he was somewhat stable, I answered.

"I guess that's who I see next. I'm not really sure."

"I'm Haney. 'Scuse my bad manners. Your name?" He reached out again for a handshake.

"I'm Laura." We shook hands. His were shaky and clammy.

"Well, if you just got here, then you're waitin' to see ol' Jeff, that male nurse right back there. I'm waitin' to see him too. Not for my first time, mind ya, but yeah, I gotta see my buddy ol' Jeff over there."

Some of the nurses were smiling and shaking their heads at Haney as they went about their work. I could see through the glass exterior wall it was getting dark outside. I must have been with that other nurse and doctor longer than I thought. It was still raining hard, and as evening turned grey to black, I thought *Dinner time. That's when it always hit me as a child.* The stomach pangs of separation, the longing for home, like a kid away at camp.

Haney continued. "I've been here since ... well, I've been here a while, but ... Hey, Ladies?" He turned toward the nurses' desks, almost toppling over again. "How long I been here?"

"You came in night before last, Haney."

Jesus Christ! And he's still drunk?"

"Right, right. That's right. Thankuverymuch, ladies," he said raising his eyebrows a bit, although his eyelids remained almost completely closed.

"So, I came in ... well, what they said." He pointed over his shoulder with his thumb. "Wait. Hey, Ladies?"

"Yes, Haney?" the older nurse answered with a smile.

"So that means I came in ..." his voice trailed off. He was looking up at the ceiling now, his fingers bouncing up and down in the air as he tried to calculate his arrival date. "That means I came in on ... oh, hold on now, just a minute. I came in on ..."

"You came in Monday night, Haney."

"Yeah, yeah. That's right. My sister, right?"

"Yes sir. Your sister brought you."

"She is a love," he said smiling to himself. "My sister. She is a love. That's a good woman right there, now. My sister." He nodded his head up and down and patted his right knee as his left hand held onto the side of his chair.

"Yes, she is," a nurse said, patting him on the shoulder as she passed through our seating area. She opened a door and disappeared down a hallway.

That's probably where the crazy people are. I can't hear them, but there's no window in that door, and it snapped shut behind her really fast. The Door to the Crazies. Wonder if they're going to put me back there.

I really didn't want to talk anymore. He was nice and all,

35

but I was feeling kind of sick. I stared at the little television in the corner of the waiting cubicle we were in. It was so small our knees were almost touching, and there was really no other place to look. I could look at Haney, which surely meant more talking, or I could stare at the television and hope he would get the hint.

"You ever been here before?"

Damn he's friendly.

"Before? Oh, no, Sir."

No, I most certainly have not been here before! Who does he think he's talking to? Is anyone watching this guy? I need a cigarette.

"Ever been *here* before?" He was wobbling in his chair again, pointing a finger down at the floor, swirling it in circles. "I mean, I know you said you never been *here* before, that's not what I meant. I heard you say that. What I meant was, you ever been in a situation like you find yourself in right now, but before." Now he was pointing around the room. "That's what I'm asking about."

I must have looked puzzled.

"Ever been rehabbed? Detoxed? Any of that?"

"Oh, no sir."

People actually do this more than once? Losers.

"Well, this is the best place to be. I can tell ya that right now, and, well, I would know. I've been around these places. This is the best right here," he said poking his finger in his chair seat. "That's what this is. Ain't that right Miss Louise?"

"What's that, Haney?" a short red-haired lady sitting at a computer answered, peeking over her bifocals.

36

"I was just telling ... what's your name again, sweetheart?"

"Laura."

"Oh yeah. Sure you are. I mean, *you sure are!*" he said laughing to himself. He patted his knee again, and then adjusted his watch. Rolex.

"That's right, Laura." Then he patted my knee. "I was just telling Laura here that this place is the best one. This is the best one, isn't it Miss Louise?"

"Yes it is, Haney. This is the best place for you to be." She gave me a wink.

"Some of these places, you know, some of them, but not all of 'em, mind ya. But some of these places just take your money and throw you in a room. Can you believe that?" He didn't wait for a response from me. "I *know* this. They take your money, throw you in a room, and you're on your own. Now that's a shame." He looked down and adjusted his watch. "Feed ya slop, too. Yeah, it's all about the money, that's what that is." He stared off into space, shaking his head.

I have nothing to say to this man! What do you say? 'Oh, hell I know it?' or what I'm really thinking, 'Oh hell! What have I gotten myself into?' He needs to stop talking to me, already. It's too much. This entire situation, it's just too much!

A tall young man came in and sat in the only other chair and began staring at his feet. He was clean cut and had a boyish face. He looked up at me when we exchanged hellos and then right back down at his feet again. He sat bent forward with his elbows on his knees. He tapped his left heel quickly, up and down, up and down and picked at his fingernails. He was wound up tight.

"I'm sorry this is taking a while." A male nurse was standing in the doorway. "If y'all will just keep being patient. Thank you." We nodded.

"If you're a smoker, you can step just outside that door right there, and there are some benches under the cover outside. You can smoke out there."

The young man and I bolted for the door, leaving Drunk Haney patting his pockets and looking on the floor underneath his chair. The two of us fired up and sat smoking in silence, but for the tap-tapping of his foot.

"How you doing?" I asked.

"I'm okay, I guess." He pulled hard on his smoke, never looking up.

"Good." Then I pulled hard on my smoke.

I realized I was staring at him, but he didn't seem to notice. He looked so young and shy. Part of me wanted to ask him what the hell happened. What could be so bad at his age to drive him to end up in this place? He was about the same age as my boys, and the bigger part of me wanted to console him, tell him everything would be all right. I wanted him to rest assured in things I myself was completely unsure of.

Instead, we sat in silence smoking and listening to the rain. The sky was really gray and sad to me, but the sound was somewhat soothing, and the smell—well, it was intoxicating! I hadn't smelled rain in months. The clouds were rolling in low and dark instead of puffy gray like before. The wind was picking up, and the happy potted plants around us were blowing side to side and bouncing up and down from the rain drops. Lush hanging baskets swayed in the breeze.

I had apparently come full circle through the medical building because I was facing the parking lot from my golf cart ride earlier. It was raining so hard I could barely see the building up on the hill where Alli had left me. I still didn't see any signs of life. There wasn't a soul in sight but the medical people inside the building behind me, Nervous Foot-tapping Guy and Drunk Haney.

I wondered where Alli was now. I patted my hip then remembered I didn't have my phone anymore. The watch I borrowed from Alli was still in my bag.

Where are my bags? I haven't seen them since I checked in. Not since Alli left. My pink bag! Had Alli's gift made it in this place? I hope she made it to my mother's house by now, changed her mind and decided to stay the night. They would be eating some dinner my mom had really made a fuss over, talking about me and my rehab. Wish I could call and check on her. I hope I have enough cigarettes. Wow! What's with this guy's tap, tap, tapping foot?

"Hey!" A bouncy, thin auburn-haired girl plopped down beside me and lit up a cigarette.

"Hi," I answered.

To say she was fair-skinned would be an understatement. I'm a fair-skinned red-head. She was translucent. Her hands trembled as she pulled hard on her smoke.

"I'm Amy," she said smiling, almost too much.

39

"I'm Laura."

"Jesse," the young man answered flatly, looking down at his tapping foot.

"Oh yeah, Jesse? What are you in here for?" Amy asked.

Well, she's wasting no time.

"Huh?" He glanced up at her then immediately back down to his feet. "Oh. Heroin." He flicked the ashes off his cigarette and bit his lip. "I do heroin."

"Really? Me too!" She was practically squealing as if they were comparing their favorite song or something.

I am not even believing this shit. How are they in here with me? Aren't they supposed to be hugging the base of a toilet, writhing on a tile floor somewhere? I mean, heroin!

"How about you, Laura? What are you in for?" Amy asked.

What am I in for? What am I, in prison now? What business is it of hers anyway?

"D.O.C.?" she pressed on. "You know, your drug of choice?"

"Oh. I don't do drugs." *Jesus, God! Why am I even near these people?*

"Oh right," she said, nodding her head. She tilted her head back, blew smoke up and stared out at the rain. "So that means you drink."

"Yeah, I drink," I mumbled under my breath. Neither of them said a word. Jesse examined his cigarette as if it were the first one he'd ever seen, rolling it between his thumb and index finger, and Amy just kept staring out at the rain.

Heroin? I still can't believe it! What if these two just flip the fuck out right here while I'm alone with them? This just doesn't seem right. They're clean, and their clothes are nice. They were making complete sentences. Heroin? There must be some kind of mistake. I just drink. And now, with the junkies right here? Not just junkies, but heroin junkies!

"Laura, he's ready for you now," Louise said leaning out of the glass door. She was barely taller than the door handle, and her blue scrubs were stretched tight over her big breasts and belly. They brushed against the door frame as she turned to waddle back to her desk.

Well, thank God! I jumped up, put out my cigarette and headed inside.

I was questioned once again about my drinking, poked and prodded in the usual medical fashion, and then asked to return to the tiny TV room. Blood pressure was way up. No surprise there. It was explained that even though I would be sleeping in the SCU for observation until I was released to a room, I would still eat in the cafeteria and participate in all day and evening activities. Tonight, however, they would have dinner delivered since I was just checking in.

Haney, Jesse and I were back together again. I had no idea where Happy Heroin Girl was. We all decided on the veal Parmesan for dinner. I was surprised by the dinner choices, and even though I wasn't really hungry, I ordered. I didn't know when they would feed me again. We stared at FoxNews in silence.

I can't retain a damn thing they're saying! I never eat dinner this early. Well, I never eat dinner. What's happening here? Tears are coming. Where did this come from?

I sipped on the water bottle I'd been given and tried to shake it off. But then, my stomach – back to the homesick place. My heart picked up its pace until I could hear it in my ears. I took a deep breath and lowered my head. Sweaty hands wringing in my lap. I needed to go somewhere, anywhere! I stood up and stared at the TV, pretending I was stretching. I couldn't understand what Shepard Smith was saying. I had to go, move, do something! I walked into the main nursing area, squeezing my dripping hands until they hurt then wiping them on my dress.

"You alright, Hon?" a nurse asked.

"Can I go smoke again?"

"Sure you can! We'll find you when your dinner gets here. Go on out there and catch you a smoke."

I could see vividly this time that the smoking area was a three-sided lattice-work enclosed area with two built-in benches facing each other. I needed to walk, so I just paced inside the small area. I didn't know if we were allowed to walk out in the parking lot area, but if we weren't, I sure didn't want a pack of nurses running after me like bloodhounds! It was pouring down rain out there anyway.

This smoking area is really small. Am I smoking too much? Will I run out of cigarettes? Would I be able to get more? Would it be like prison in here with the cigarettes?

I was calculating how many days my smokes would last when someone's voice crept into my thoughts.

"Laura! Telephone for you!"

"Wha? For me?"

It was Jeff, patting me on the shoulder. "Someone's been looking for you!" he said smiling.

"Huh?" I quickly looked around. *What the hell?* Somehow, I was now in Jeff's cubicle with a blood pressure cuff on my right arm. I had no idea how I got there or the time of day. I quickly glanced to my right. It was pitch black outside.

"Your husband! He's been calling all over campus looking for you!"

Ol' Jeff's awfully fired up about this phone call! I never dreamed I would be talking to Leroy today. I don't know what to say. I feel so heavy. So very, very heavy. I really don't want to talk to anyone.

Jeff showed me the phone in the tiny TV room. Haney was passed out with his head back against the wall with his mouth wide open, letting out an occasional apnea-like snort. Jesse was still tapping that left foot up and down, staring at the floor. *Oh perfect. I'll just take this potentially emotional phone call right here in between the knees of Drunk Haney and Heroin Boy. Shit.*

"Excuse me, please." I inched past Haney's knees. He let out a snort, smacked his lips and went right on sleeping. Jeff transferred the call.

"Hello?"

"Hey, Babe! You all right?" Leroy said, trying to sound upbeat, but I could feel the concern in his voice. My heart hurt for all I had put him through, and now this! He doesn't sleep well when I'm away. Whenever I would return from a trip, my side of

43

the bed would still look freshly made, but for the wrinkles at the bottom where his leg had been sweeping my side so he could feel me next to him. Why he would even want me there anymore, I don't know.

"Yeah, I'm okay." *Well that didn't sound convincing.* I cleared my throat and tried again. "Yes! I'm okay!" I tried to muster some sense of enthusiasm. I didn't want him worrying.

"You sure? Things going all right? You feel like you've done the right thing?"

"Oh yeah. For sure." That was the truth.

"You sure, Babe? You're okay?"

"Yeah, I am okay. I'm sure."

"Mom?" *Oh my God, it's Matt. I've got to sound better than this!*

Matt, our youngest, had come home from college to be with his dad. He was playing football and studying to be a coach. He had been so thrilled when I called to tell him I was going to Rehab. He was a sweet, sweet soul.

"Hey, Bear!" I tried to clean up my act, like when he was little and I was sick.

"Mom, you okay?"

"Yes, I'm good!" My voice was cracking. *I'm feeling too much. It's all just too much. My chest may explode!*

"Do you think you can do this, Mama?"

"Oh yeah, I got this, I ..."

"I mean, I *know* you can do this, Mom." He had caught himself with the "if" talk. I'd taught him well.

"I'm good. I'm just tired. That's all it is. I'm just really tired."

"I love you, Mom. This is good. I'm so happy for you. I love you."

Well, hell, that's it. Tears are coming now.

"Thanks, Bear. I promise I'm okay. Everyone has been very nice to me. They are nice people, I ... well ... I gotta go now. Please don't worry. Promise me you won't worry."

"Okay, Mom. It's all gonna be all right."

"I know it is. It's going be better soon. I know it is. I'm going to work hard. I love you, Bear. I love you," I said, my voice quivering and trailing off.

"I love you too, Mama." And I knew my big six foot two, three hundred ten pound baby boy was crying. My sweet, sweet, Bear.

"Laura?" It was Leroy again. I didn't want him to know I was crying. "Babe? You sure you're okay?"

"Oh yeah, I'm good. I'm just really tired. It's been a long day."

"It really has! You left here a long time ago, and I've thought about you all day. But you're okay? Feeling like you did the right thing in this?"

"Yes. Don't worry about that at all. I did, and I know it. Everyone has been very nice to me. It's just that, well, there's no privacy where I am right now. I just ... I need to go, okay?"

"Okay, Baby. I love you. I'm so proud of you. Get some rest."

"I love you too. I'll find out what the deal is with the phones and call you soon, okay?"

"Okay. I love you, Laura."

"Love you too."

*   *   *

It seemed days or weeks had already passed since our goodbye in the wee morning hours that same day, and for me, much more than miles had already been covered. I had loaded my things in the car that morning with all the efficiency and routine of packing for yet another game day trip for one of our kid's athletic events, and when I was done, I paused in the carport, hands on hips, and took a new look at our old house. I shook it off and came back in to find Leroy standing in our bedroom, his mouth forming that upside down smile that keeps him from crying. It felt like such betrayal leaving him to seek help from outsiders.

"I'm so sorry," I whispered. "I'm sorry for everything, but now I'm really sorry for going so far away."

"Baby, I would take you down there, but with the company sale just a few days away, I ..."

"I told you I think it's the smart thing to do. What you're doing is the right thing. I made all these plans without you, anyway, and there's nothing you need to do for me right now. Come see me later. Come see me when I'm better. And I will be better. Somehow, I just know it."

"I know you will. It's good. This is a good thing, but I will miss you so much."

"I'm so sorry." I could hardly bear looking at him.

He pulled my head to his chest, wrapped himself all around me and tried to whisper through his cracking voice, "I know. Don't be sorry. This is good. I'll miss you, but this is good." I pulled away, held his face in my hands and felt his warm tears streaming over my fingers. We locked eyes on each other, and I left.

Despite the sense of betrayal, I had left him. Left him for strangers attempting to recover from my alcohol abuse. Left him alone in the convoluted position of attempting to recover from living with me, then adjusting to living without me.

I didn't know if I believed he would miss me. Who could long to be with the person I had become? *Manage, manipulate, control. Manipulate that situation. Control these people. Never solving anything but always resolving to. Never making things right, but making them right for right now.* And then one day, for no apparent reason, and with no explanation to him, it was time to stop putting out fires. *This fucker is burning down!* A part of me wondered if he could still love me after the before, and then after whatever the hell was about to happen. Could we get it back to good? But the larger part, the autopilot, didn't allow those thoughts or feelings for long. I realize now it was the shutting down that saved me. The insanity had to stop.

And now it was done and ready or not, here I was. I could hardly bear it. The weight of my shame, the agonizing remorse. I ached for what I was putting my family through. I fell back in my chair and put my face in my hands. The wailing that brewed inside me would not escape, though. My tightening chest and throat made sure of that. My body shook from the pressure of holding it all in. Never before had I cried so deeply, so quietly. No one around me said a word.

*   *   *

It was explained to me initially in SCU and then repeatedly thereafter that I was never to allow myself to become uncomfortable or agitated during my detox. "And never, *absolutely never*, allow yourself to go without sleep. We can help you in a safe, non-addictive way." You're here to get well, they would say, and you can't get well without rest.

My things had been delivered to SCU sometime while I was in with the doctor. I knew they were mine because, although they were no longer in my bag, I could see all my stuff sitting right there in the tiny lobby in clear, crinkly plastic bags. There were several other bags stacked outside Jeff's office. Jeff checked the tags, picked up my two bags and set them outside the windowless Doorway to the Crazies.

"I'll get those for you, Hon, and show you where your bed is," one of the female nurses said to me.

"Oh, I can carry my own bags, no need for that."

"You'll have enough work to do in time, so let me do this for you," she said as she got up from her desk. Then we passed through the door with no window, and I felt short of breath.

The room was dimly lit and seemed to have a blue haze around the edges. The floor was blue tile, then there were white sheets, white blankets, white pillows ... everywhere, white. *Like a loony bin. Wow.*

She placed my things on the floor beside the third bed on

the left. There was a small dresser at the foot of the bed and otherwise the area was like any hospital E.R. or semi-private room. There were light blue curtains to pull around the bed for privacy, a night stand (no remote control) and a pull-string light on the wall behind the head of the bed. I froze at the side of the bed.

"This will be your bed, Hon," the nurse said smiling. "Just for a little while until you move to a room. You okay?"

Hell if I know. I shrugged, and began digging for my night clothes. *Hmm. See-through plastic bags, lots of white. I guess that's what people like me get.*

It was obvious someone had gone through my things, and the clear plastic was a way to indicate to the staff that my stuff was, non-threatening, or whatever it is they needed to know about people like me. I wondered what they'd taken from my bags after inspection. I'd been very meticulous in my packing to make sure I followed the rules. I referred to the checklist online. No electronic devices whatsoever, no shirts with drug or alcohol themes (outgrew those a while back) and no lewd clothing or two-piece bathing suits (I'm a forty-nine year-old mother of three.) I made sure I packed non-alcohol mouthwash, and I'd turned in my prescription drugs at check-in.

I really wanted to shower, but the lights were low, and the room was quiet, so I dug out my night clothes, slipped them on, and went to the bathroom to brush my teeth. Two other women were rustling through their bags getting ready for bed too, and we all moved about our bedtime rituals exchanging nods and whispered pleasantries.

Like a hotel, the bathroom had a wide vanity counter and separate area for the toilet and shower. When I laid my things on the vanity and stepped into the shower room looking for a towel and wash cloth, school gym came to mind, and I decided I was perfectly okay with a decent freshen up and change of clothes. Brushing my teeth, I leaned back against the vanity hoping my eyes had adjusted to the light so I could get a full take on the room. That's when the *déjà vu* hit. I had heard that door close behind me, seen the blue curtains flowing around the beds, felt the cold of the tile beneath my feet. *That's impossible! I'm just tired. It's just been a very long, strange day.* My throat tightened, and I thought I might puke, so I quickly turned to spit in the sink and rinse my mouth. Another squinted scan of the room, and I knew the familiar feelings were very real. I had indeed, been in this place before – much earlier in this very long, very strange day.

*　　*　　*

Doors had closed firmly behind us, and then curtains were pulled around us.

"I need you to pull your underwear down and your dress and bra up, please," the nurse said. My eyes shot first to hers in disbelief then down to the floor. When my heavy head dropped, tears rushed right up to the edges of my closed eyelids, and my throat tightened.

So it's come to this.

I slowly raised my head and complied while she smiled apologetically. "Now step out of your underwear, please. Oh, bless

50

your heart, you're a little shaky there, dear." She gently lifted my heavy arm and placed it on her shoulder for support. I pointed my chin towards the ceiling to drain the tears back into my head, because you know what happens if just one slips through. My face burned red, then I heard the swoosh of all my blood leaving, and I went cold.

"Do you need to sit down?" the nurse asked, gently holding my arm.

"No. I'm fine ... I think. Yeah, I'm fine. Really."

The other nurse dumped my purse onto the vanity counter and meticulously searched through the contents. She opened my water bottle and gave it a sniff. She pulled out what few bills I had and ran her fingers through every pocket and crevice in my wallet. She poured out the coins and began tapping them on the counter. She would tap a coin, inspect the counter, wipe it clean, and start over again with the next coin.

How many times have I told these people that I only drink? I don't have a freakin' DOC. I have a damn drinking problem, that's all! This is horrifying! What does she think, I'm some kind of coke addict?

"Oh, I can't afford that stuff," I joked. The nurse smiled and went on with her coin-tapping. She took out my magazine, flipped through the pages and then shook it over the vanity. She turned my entire purse inside out, threw away random vitamins and tiny pieces of paper, patted it down and then turned it right side in again.

"Sorry about all this," she said. The EKG would be next, she had explained and then escorted me back to the cubicle with the tiny TV.

*   *   *

But now I was dressed for bed and looking forward to sitting alone, writing in my new journal. There was a lot to write about, and I didn't want to forget a single thing. A nurse came back and strapped a monitor on my arm. This allowed them to monitor my vitals while I slept. That way, she said, they wouldn't have to disturb me in the night, and the beeping and buzzing wouldn't keep me awake.

I got out my journal and pen and began fluffing up my pillows and covers for some comfy writing. Another nurse came in to explain lights out. We were welcome to quietly read or write in our bed with our wall lights on, but the overhead lights were to be out.

I felt cozy writing behind my curtain walls with the backlighting behind me. It was strange to feel so comfortable in a room so similar to an E.R. I pondered that for a bit, and decided that it was appropriate enough. I hadn't written anything in years. I thought about it occasionally, but it was quickly dismissed. "What's the point? I'm a grown woman who has to make a living!" and more often, "What if someone finds it and reads it? I have kids, for God's sake!" And when I was finally deep into my drinking, I had a conscious fear of what might fill the pages, knowing that once written, such things become very real and undeniable. Couldn't have that. Too murky.

I began writing vigorously. Haney, the rehab frequent-flier.

Amy and Jesse, the heroin addicts. The kind, but persistent staff with their endless questions about the stuff nobody talks about. And me, forced to face the truth—my truth. There was something big happening here. So big I was much too tired to ponder it in any meaningful way. But somehow, right in the middle of the overwhelmingly unknown, confusing shit of it all, I knew. I began my journaling.

> **It's summer 2011, and I've finally had enough of me – checked myself into rehab. Well, I called them, and then the rehab people talked to the insurance people, and they decided I was both drunk enough and insured enough to go, so here I am. What have I done? We shall see. There's all this new jargon, all this talking, talking, talking about stuff no one talks about. It's exhausting. I'm exhausted.**

"You *know,* some people want to sleep around here!" Amy yelled from the front of the room. She was in the first bed, and I recognized her voice. No one said a word or even moved. I had no idea what time it was, and I had no way to check because I had no phone and had yet to find the watch I borrowed from Alli.

"C'mon, people! You know it's late if I'm ready to sleep. Shit!" Amy rustled her covers and pounded her pillows. "Goddammit!"

Oh God! My heart was racing. I strained my eyes to see if anyone else was up. A light quickly went off in another sheet box up front by Amy, but still no one moved or spoke. Mine was the lone light now. *Oh God! Amy was a heroin addict! Was she going to flip out in here tonight?* I imagined her violently pulling back her curtains with her auburn hair flying in all directions. Her long, white, skinny legs would be flailing out of her hospital gown and off the bed as she threw things, and nurses and orderlies tried to restrain her.

Oh God! What am I doing here with these people? Do I call for help? Is there even a call button in here? What should I do? I wanted to journal. With all my heart, I wanted to journal so as not to lose one morsel of this extraordinary day. But even more, I didn't want her flipping out while nurses in crisp white uniforms swarmed the room and bed pans clanged on the floor.

Our nurses didn't even wear white uniforms, there wasn't a single bed pan in our little ward, and no one was wearing a hospital gown either. Nevertheless, in my mind, that's how it was going down, so I quickly wrapped my journal in some clothes and pushed the bundle way down in my clear luggage. I couldn't have these kinds of people looking through my things, much less reading my private thoughts and feelings. I felt like an adolescent girl hiding her diary or a naive new prison inmate. *There's probably some drug-head bully who would tease me about keeping a diary or beat my ass if she were mentioned in it.* I adjusted the monitor on my arm and turned off my light.

I stared at the blue-tinted ceiling, down at my crisp, white sheets, and then back at the ceiling. I tried to process the day. Saying goodbye to Leroy and then Alli. Then I thought about how happy Matt had been when I called and told him I was going to Rehab. "Mom, you have just made me so happy. I'm so proud of you." And how our oldest had been surprisingly speechless. We had always had good honest conversations, and all he had for me was dumbfounded silence. I could feel him wanting to escape the conversation completely. It worried me at first, but then, though I hate to admit it, it had been easy to let go. By that point, I was so flat I couldn't hang on to anything or anyone for long. I knew he would support me because my drinking had been the subject of one of those honest conversations many months before.

* * *

"I love you, Mom. You know that. And I'm not saying you lost your job because of it, but this could be a good chance for you to start over. Quit drinking, you know? There are a lot of people who care about you who would help. I bet you can get in one of those AA groups around here. You know people who have sobered up around here, right?"

I just stared back. *I can't even believe this conversation is taking place. My own son, talking to me like this! When did everything get so backwards, so messed up?*

"I'm not threatening you, Mom. And I'm not bribing you either. I want you to get better. But after I'm married? When we start having kids? This guy ... this guy is not having his kids around this. This is not happening."

"I understand. I understand, and I'll do better. Thank you." I was sitting on the edge of my bed, looking down, because I couldn't bear to look him in the eye. I could see a drink I had hidden underneath the end table.

"Whew!" he said. "So, we're good?"

"Yeah, we're good."

"Okay!" he said laughing. "Wow, okay. I mean, I'd really worked myself up thinking this was going to be really bad, you yelling mad and everything, you know?"

"It's not bad. I hear you, and we're okay." I smiled through clenched jaws. The shame welling up vibrated my insides so fiercely I feared my teeth would chatter. We really were okay, because I wasn't angry at all. I was terrified.

I didn't drink at all for two or three days after that though I thought of little else. Stressful day, blah, blah, blah. Let the rationalizations begin. I decided I could drink a little wine to take the edge off in the evening, no harm done. But I couldn't drink a little of anything anymore, and there wasn't enough wine in the world to get me comfortable anyway. In less than a week, I crawled back up on that dark horse, and I rode the hell out of that son of a bitch for one more long, tortuous, heart-breaking year.

*   *   *

Now I was in a hospital where neither friends nor family, cards or calls are received. I had no experience to draw from – there was no baby to be born, no surgery pending. *I was pending.* I lay in my white room for what seemed like five or more hours, and sleep wouldn't come. But fear, shame and regret did. They always came at night.

Head Traffic. *Life's review of my regrets and indignation. Remorse and self-righteous justifications. Words I wish I could snatch back and swallow. My best intentions, never executed. Starting with a low, barely-audible hum, joined by shallow breath and the vibrating beat of my heart. Then as the tempo and volume increase, the swoosh of blood flying past my ears on its way to my temples. The mental and the physical smashed together like a time-lapse video that takes a frantic city from morning to noon to night in less than sixty seconds.*

I am above the traffic. Individuals and scenes flashing in and out of view. But even as quickly as they come and go, I recognize the people and the places and the pain is fresh, and it comes to stay. They remain discernable until the fast forward of the day brings long-fingered shadows that crawl across the pavement, slither up skyscrapers and over the top, then pour over on to another sidewalk. One after the other the shadows come, so rapidly, so closely, until finally flashes of daylight can no longer squeeze between them and darkness seals the final seam. Signals for me to stop have given way to strobe-like yellow flashes of warning, and the distinctions seen in daylight are now serpentine smears of red and white lights rushing to on ramps and off ramps and into the arteries that go on forever. Stillness. Silence. My breathy sigh of relief in my ears. Then I am jolted into the darkness.

I am in the traffic. Bottlenecked so tightly and pushed along so rapidly, it is impossible to view what lies of ahead of me and any opportunity to exit has passed before I see it. Behind me, more opportunities to exit missed by me as I force my way through the streaks of red and white, leaving them mired and off course. Chaos. The tangled wreckage behind, the squeezing bottleneck, the blur ahead – the pace and thickness of it all fills me with panic. Destination, unknown. And I am on the brink of forgetting where it is I came from.

Head traffic. The time lapse of my life every goddamn night.

Chapter 6

Although this, my first night in Rehab was certainly new, the restlessness was nothing new at all. There was strange comfort in not having to lie to myself about what was really going on, and why. My body needed a drink.

It's surely four-thirty or five o'clock by now. I stared at the ceiling. I searched for the light that kept the blue tint alive in the otherwise dark room. I wished for the light at the head of my bed, but I didn't dare turn it on for fear of the now *Un*happy Heroin Girl. I surveyed my curtain walls for shadows of other patients who might possibly be awake too. No movement.

I've got to be up at six. I won't be able to function tomorrow ... today, whatever. Hell, I can't take it anymore!

I finally gave up and got up.

I felt around on the floor, found my flip-flops and slipped them on. My legs were heavy and tight. They felt like they were pushing through mud as I shuffled toward the windowless door and into the nursing area. My clothes were sticking to every sweaty part of my body they could grab. I rubbed my tight, damp neck and hoped my thick, curly hair didn't look light-socket crazy. *Who cares? I've got to get some sleep.* I shuffled into the nursing area, squinted from the bright lights and finally found a clock. It was two-thirty.

"Oh thank God," I mumbled, looking down to be sure I was completely covered. A v-shaped sweat mark ran from my neck to my stomach. I felt the dampness of the back of my head and the small of my back. My entire body was so damp and heavy. The monitor hung off my elbow as if the strap were about to give up.

"Oh thank God," I repeated with a gasp.

"What is it, Hon?"

I had no idea who was speaking to me. My eyes hadn't adjusted to the light, and all the nurses I could see were new to me, or at least I thought they were. A male nurse stepped out of a corner office. He wore brown scrubs and cowboy boots. He was definitely new.

"What is it, Laura?" *How does he know my name?*

"Well, see ... I thought for sure it had to be five-thirty or six, and I haven't slept ... like, haven't slept at all. Thank God I've still got time. I mean, just look at me." I pulled at my sweaty shirt and ran my fingers through the back of my hair. "I can't sleep. I'm soaking wet."

He sat on the corner of a desk and smiled. He had a nice face. "We can help you with the sleeping for sure, but the sweating? Can't really do anything for you there. Sorry, but that sweating is really the best thing you can do to get all that out of your system."

I pulled my shirt away from my skin, fanned it against my body and pointed to a chart on the desk beside him. "Well, then," I said, pausing to clear my throat. "Let the record reflect that I'm most certainly doing my part because I'm sweating my ass off over here." They all laughed, and I was grateful for the tension-breaker because this scene was beyond surreal. Me, in this place, having this conversation. I shook my head in disbelief.

"Let me check your chart, and we'll help you out, Laura. We'll get you some sleep."

"That's right," another nurse said. "And you did the right thing. We want you to get your sleep. Don't ever just lay there and go without sleep. It's not good for you."

"Thank you. Thank you very much. Can I still step outside to smoke this late?"

"Sure you can. Just come see me when you come back in, and I'll fix you up."

There was a zombie in pajamas slumped in a chair by the door, and she pulled a cigarette and lighter from her pack and held them straight up without even looking at me. I took them, thanked her and stepped outside.

I believe I'm officially detoxing from alcohol. Ain't that some shit.

I took a couple of drags before it occurred to me that I might not want to smoke a cigarette from a zombie chick in rehab, even if it had saved me a couple of steps, so I put it out and stepped back in to the SCU.

"Come on over here and let me help you get some sleep," a nurse said, holding a bottle of water and a pill cup.

I'm going to be okay. I think I'm going to be okay.

61

Chapter 7

My memory of the first two or three days of detoxing is black and white with jolts and bright flashes of white, like an old eight millimeter film. And while some parts are more clear than others, most are more like snapshots or vague blurs than actual recollections. Though it never rained again after that first day, I saw my new home through foggy eyes for several more days. Everything on campus, from the plants to the people, were now simply varying shades of gray with few distinguishing characteristics.

Maybe it was the enormity of admitting I couldn't fix something so horribly wrong with me, no matter how hard I'd tried. Maybe it was the humbling experience of having finally thrown in the towel and called for help. It could have been that I was detoxing. The cause was of little import, really. The fact was, I was a zombie now, moving robotically through my days, somehow pushing through one and on to the next.

Strangers gently guided and encouraged me along my way as needed during those early days by checking the schedule I dutifully carried in my folder and showing me where I needed to be, or by simply calling my name and wishing me a good day. "How you doing today, Laura? Things going all right so far?" one Community member might ask me as we gathered for a large group meeting or as we passed on the sidewalk. I had no idea how they knew my name and no mental capacity to be curious about it for more than the brief moment it took for them to speak.

There were so many of them, and they didn't seem to grasp the seriousness of the situation. *They probably belong here and know it.* I had left my home, where I cooked dinner. My town, where people knew me. My job, where I worked my ass off. Do they not realize the tragedy this is for me? The Community, they were called, not patients. *The Community. Bunch of bad alcoholics and even drug addicts, for God's sake!*

"Laura, this lady will show you where your Newcomer Group meets. We know all these limestone buildings with their red metal roofs look alike. Anyone will help you, anytime. But she's going to show you where to go right now."

The Community, with their scrambled faces and noisy static, moved around me and past me, and the staff in my detox unit, all looking the same with their silver hair, scrubs and tennis shoes, who probably thought I was some lazy, terrible drunk, and who surely had no comprehension of my difficulties. They all pushed and prodded me like cattle, insisting that I stay awake and moving.

I dragged myself through those early days. It felt like hot lava was oozing through my veins, down my legs and pooling in my heavy feet. I kept my eyes on the ground when shuffling across campus, partially for balance, mostly for isolation. In class, I opened my materials then studied my nervous, sweaty hands, twitching on my lap.

I had some sense of God's presence in the darkness, but it wasn't like some needlepoint Footprints poetry. The lone, deep footprints were mine as He stood by and watched me drag myself through each day, burning and aching inside and out. He had to let me burn and ache so I could learn to feel again. I now know, He waited for the very last remaining part of me to burn and crumble away, because when my pride was finally gone, He could build me back up into the Me He had always intended.

*   *   *

One of the nurses took me up the large hill from SCU in a golf cart to a morning meeting. She had come to my bedside earlier that morning as I sat staring down at my feet. I felt lost and so very alone.

I guess I should put shoes on, but I don't know what I'm doing next. Am I going somewhere? Do I ask? Or do I just sit in here like in any other hospital room and wait for people to come to me?

"Hon? You ready to get on up there to the morning meeting?"

"Oh. I guess. I don't know. Is that what I'm supposed to do?"

"That's what you need to be doing." She patted my shoulder. "You get those shoes on, and I'll run you up there to the Community meeting so you won't be late."

"Yes ma'am." I was so relieved someone told me what to do next.

She drove me up the hill and parked the golf cart beside a

walkway leading to the largest stone building with a red metal roof. Stragglers rushed across the large patio and into the doorway.

"That door right there on the end," she said pointing. I sat frozen. "Go on," she said, waving her hand for me to get out of the cart. "We'll see you after while." She gave me a warm encouraging smile, so me and my lead feet reluctantly trudged up the sidewalk and into the building.

Everyone's looking at me. This sucks. I feel like a little kid.

I remember sitting near the back, close to the doors and windows. I don't remember much at all about that meeting. Bunch of people saying they were alcoholics and addicts, some loud guy at the front talking and talking and *talking*. Some people were laughing, and an older lady patted me on the shoulder as she headed to her seat. All of it was cloaked in gray, and even though most of the sound was muffled, it was still too much. I looked out the windows at the cloudy skies and gray concrete sidewalks. I cried softly and wondered what the hell I was crying about. But this cry was bossy and demanding. This cry was taking place, and I had no say about it. There was simply no stuffing it. I returned to the SCU after the meeting, my back and legs aching so, I was angry with pain. I had been rear-ended at a red light about a week before I went into Rehab, and my back had been bothering me quite a bit. I was sure that was the reason for my fatigue and irritability. I had taken my prescription pain medication with me to Rehab, explained the reason for the medication and turned them in at check-in, all according to instructions. I wanted to reassure them that pills weren't my thing, I had truly been injured, and that even a doctor had said my pain was genuine, in case I needed something later. All of that was true.

"Excuse me, Ma'am?" I stood in front of Miss Verna's desk. She was the head battle-ax. I had this figured out.

"Well, hello, Laura! Back so soon? Don't you have somewhere you're supposed to be?"

"My back is hurting, and ..."

"Oh, here, have a seat," she said patting the chair next to her desk. "Now, go on, Hon."

"Well, my back is hurting, and now it's making my legs feel really tired. I was wondering if I could have something for the pain."

"Okay. Let me check your chart just a minute." She shuffled through files on her desk. Mine was still handy because I was still living in the SCU, and I was in and out throughout the day for blood pressure checks. Doctor's orders.

"See, I had a car wreck," I continued as she flipped through my file.

"Related to your drinking?" she asked. "Had you been drinking?"

"Well, no. Well, yes, I had been drinking, but that's not the issue right now. Someone rear-ended me, a while before I came, and I brought my meds down here, when I checked in, you know. And turned them in like it said, but now I ..."

"I don't see any order for pain medication in here, Laura, but I can contact the doctor for you."

So this is how it's going to be. Everyone's going to assume I'm some kind of drug addict because I have a drinking problem. They don't even know me! This is crap. I'm hurting, and she doesn't even give a damn.

"You don't believe me," I said quietly, hanging my heavy head down.

"No, Laura. I just said I would have to contact the doctor to see if we can give you anything because there's nothing mentioned in your chart."

"You think I'm lying!" I slapped my hands down on my thighs (which hurt) and then stood. "Well, this is just great!" I stormed out of the waiting area, whipped open the Door to the Crazies, and marched back to my bed, but my momentum was quickly stalled. The curtain around my bed was hung up on the dresser, and the head of my bed was still raised, with my pillow pinched in the metal frame. *Every single thing in this place is so fuckin' tedious! Can't even throw a decent fit!* I lowered the head of my bed, tossed my pillow to the top, pulled the curtain out of my dresser drawer and then around my bed, and finally, plopped face-down for a good ol' pissed-off female cry. I have no idea how long I laid there. I remember later that day standing in front of the bathroom mirror washing my face and internally declaring the episode over. It was time to move on.

* * *

"You doing okay, Laura?" Jenny was leaning on the dresser at the end of my bed. She was a pretty blonde thirty-something mom of two small boys. Her wardrobe had failed to adjust to her changing body, so she was always a bit squished into whatever trendy clothing she wore.

I was sitting on the side of my bed, struggling to get my sneakers on because my heavy legs were so tight they wouldn't bend, or my back was so tight I couldn't bend over enough. I wasn't sure what the problem was.

"I'm all right, I guess."

"Well, good news here!" she said. "They're moving Theresa and me into a room today!"

What the hell?

Jenny and Theresa checked in the morning of the same day I arrived. They had both been very nice to me, and I had hoped Jenny would be my roommate. I had been nervous about the rooming situation even before I got there.

"I'm old," I'd told Alli. "I don't make friends as easily as I used to." Alli had laughed me off and said, "Don't worry, Mom. Everyone likes you."

"What?" I asked Jenny. I stopped struggling with my shoes and stared blankly up at her. "Both of you get to leave? You *and* Trese?"

"Yes," Jenny laughed. "Theresa and I are both out of here, girl. Moving to a real room!"

I knew why she was laughing. I hadn't pronounced Theresa's name correctly since we met. I had no idea what my problem was there. I didn't mean to be rude, but I honestly couldn't keep it in my head, and if it was in my head, I couldn't make my mouth say it right. But I couldn't worry about that right now because there were much stranger things going on.

Theresa strolled over near my bed grinning. She was closer to my age, mid-forties was my guess, and she had two sons in college. Her tanned, skinny frame held up her white t-shirt like a wire hanger. "You hear our good news?" she asked. But when she saw my face, she quickly lost her smile and said, "I'm sorry. I didn't mean to be rude. They'll move you soon. Don't be sad."

Pissed off would be a better description. "Well, I don't mean to be a party pooper. I'm glad for y'all. Really, I am."

This is so messed up! Something is so very wrong here! How the hell could they be released to a room before me? If any woman in here should get released, it's me! I only drink, after all. Look at these people they've put me with in here! They pop pills, smoke dope. There were two heroin addicts in here, for God's sake! Where is the logic in all of that? And these two chicks, pill poppers who drink and smoke pot too, getting moved out of here ahead of me? Xanax Housewives. It's bullshit.

I was indignant! I felt I had failed, but by no fault of my own. This had to be a mistake! More likely, some nurse was out to get me. *Bitches. Don't they have anything better to do than make my life a further living hell?* Well, yes they actually did.

Later I would come to understand that I, in all my internally self-proclaimed awesomeness – a mere drinker, by the way – was more likely to die from detox than anyone else in there. Those nurses whom I perceived as clueless and vindictive were actually closely following a doctor's orders, and doing their damnedest to not only keep me alive and well, but even comfortable in my detox! I hadn't done a damn thing to deserve that courtesy. I was later informed by one of my addict friends, "Your DOC may be legal, but alcohol's some serious shit in detox." I didn't know.

How and when did this happen? When did I start aimlessly driving around in the afternoons after work, afraid to go home and be alone? When did it become so difficult for me to take care of myself or my home? When was that first morning I woke up and left the house as fast as I could because things were already spinning too fast? More importantly, on what day did I wake up and decide I needed to have a drink before anything else could take place?

Chapter 8

Any smaller group I attended during those first days was filled with other newcomers, and meetings were held in a small building off the beaten path of the main campus. "All these stone buildings look alike. Stone buildings everywhere with red roof tops," someone said. She walked me to the smaller building and stood next to me in the doorway while my eyes adjusted to the dark room. Down two steps, turn right, and down three more. I surveyed the long, empty room. Chairs were placed in a large circle, some with folders and books on the seat, others without. Narrow, rectangular windows lined the right side, dark wood paneling down the left. It felt like a basement because the windows were level with the backs of the chairs. There was another door at the far end, and a tall blonde woman in a white linen dress floated through it and into the room.

"Hi, Laura! Welcome!"

"Hello," I answered, still perusing the room. I felt lost, but she had called me by name, so, I figured I must be in the right place.

"You'll need to take one of the chairs with the literature in them. You'll find a folder with your current schedule and some other paperwork. That's an AA Big Book on top. We'll discuss those in more detail a little later."

I took a chair opposite the wall with the windows and purposefully placed the literature on my lap. *Now what?*

The lady in white was obviously our group leader. I watched her organizing books and folders, but when she looked up, I glanced away or looked down at my reading materials. She was a heavy-set woman with a bobbed hairstyle. She wore no makeup and lots of big jewelry. *Left over hippie.* She kept tossing her head to get her bangs out of her eyes, and when she did, her clunky jewelry rattled like pocket change.

Other people began to filter in. The flowy lady in white smiled and greeted the group as she began the meeting. Her name was Carla. She instructed each member of the group to introduce themselves (no last names) and state their DOC.

Now this? Just when I thought I couldn't feel more awkward.

I was edgy, constantly shifting my weight, adjusting my sandals, crossing and uncrossing my legs and whatever else I could find to do. I glanced around the room, but never made eye contact.

There were equal numbers of young and old, and more women than men in our group. Frequent Flier Haney was there, but he was already nodding off like an old man in church. Amy, Jenny and Theresa from SCU were there. As instructed, each introduced themselves and identified their DOC.

"Hi guys. I'm Amy, and I use intravenous heroin." She had such an ease to her, she was almost cocky.

"Jesse. Drug addict." Tap tap tap goes the left foot.

"Jenny. Xanax and alcohol."

"I am Theresa. I smoke pot, and I drink. Oh! I take Xanax, too!" she giggled.

Idiot. "Laura. Alcohol."

And on and on, until each of the fifteen or so of us had introduced ourselves and our problem.

We were taught AA Meeting decorum, and some very basic group therapy guidelines. Don't hug, pat or even touch another group member when they become emotional. This can cause the person sharing to shut down, and if they cut short their share, perhaps limiting their processing, we were told. No passing of tissues for the same reasons. If the person sharing wants a tissue, he or she can get one. There will be plenty placed around the room. I was never much for navel gazing, self-reflection, whatever. This was all new to me.

We were to speak only in first person, and only discuss, analyze, or critique our own issues. No cross talk in response to what another has shared, and speak only of your own experience. Be respectful. No talking, whispering, or excessive noise or activity, such as moving your study materials or rustling papers while someone else is speaking. I settled a bit further into my chair and tried to become invisible, studiously leafing through my handouts.

The Newcomer Group was fluid, so the number of members would vary from day to day. New people would flow in and receive instructions and assignments, and those who had completed the required work would flow out, moving on to the next level of their Recovery. Carla said one of the requirements was for each member to write a Goodbye Letter to their DOC. She paused afterward to let that sink in. The new people were given guidelines as to what was to be included, and I gave it a glance and stuffed it away in my folder.

A Goodbye Letter to alcohol? Really? What a bunch of kindergarten bullshit. I'll smoke this assignment, blow her socks off and move forward in record time.

"And then you will read it aloud to the group," Carla said.

Oh ... well ... now, wait just a minute. There are probably fifteen or twenty people in here! People I don't even know. Don't see what good can come of that. It's bullshit.

"And today, Amy is ready to read her Goodbye Letter to the group," Carla said smiling and turning to Amy. Everyone closed their materials and locked their eyes on Amy, and I followed their lead.

She began her reading with a brief background of her introduction to drugs and alcohol in the party scene. Then came her slippery slide into drug abuse and finally, the horrific tale of her intravenous heroin addiction. She told of days on end looking for the next fix. No food, no shower, no sleep. Just fixated on the fix. There was nothing too filthy or compromising if it would get her what she needed to get right, she said.

She read. She screamed and cursed. She cried. Her body shook like nothing I'd seen before. Her chest was heaving so, I feared she might pass out, and the ragged sides of her paper, torn from a spiral notebook, flopped up and down as her hands trembled.

I was mesmerized.

She cleared her throat and wiped her drenched face on her crisp, long-sleeved shirt, then sat up straight with new resolve. "And so, in conclusion, I say goodbye to you, heroin," she read. "You're the devil. I'm sure of it because you've taken everything. My family, my future ... even the *me* I used to know. You took it all! *Every* fuckin' thing that matters, you hear me?" she shouted with tears streaming down her thin, drawn face. Then she hung her head until her chin was on her chest, and with quivering lips, just above a whisper, she uttered, "Adios, you motherfucker. I'm done."

No one drew a breath. There was no air in the room to breathe. And with trembling hands, she tightly folded her pages over and over into a small square, mashed them firmly between her palms and passed them down to our leader.

I internally noted the irony of the scene, her passing a note like that *to* the teacher. And though all the horrible mess that was her life and the dark secrets she had dragged through that mess were now out there all naked and raw, how she had meticulously folded her pages over and over themselves as if to keep the sad truth of the words inside from spilling out again. Those pages contained more pain, struggle and shame than any girl her age should ever have to know. She should be passing notes about dates and dresses, I thought to myself.

Most everyone in the group was wiping away tears, and we all looked like someone had punched us in the gut as we sat with our heads down and hands clasped tightly on our laps. I felt as if I had witnessed someone torturing herself. It was so brutal and jagged that when I finally did glance up at her, I almost expected to see slashes and bruising. But she just sat there all skinny and pale, limp with exhaustion.

I sat stunned in the silence. I had two days to work on the assignment.

That night, I read the assignment outline and set out to write the most articulate, well-organized, grammatically correct Goodbye Letter ever in the history of Rehab. What I ended up with was an emotional chronicle of my very close, very lengthy relationship with alcohol. One that started as a party, disintegrated into just plain pathetic, and now was ending with a bitter breakup demand by me. My anger towards my dear old friend surprised me. It was as if I had been plucked from a sick relationship, and only in that removal could I begin to see it for what it really was. My life partner alcohol had become a selfish sonofabitch:

> *"No one new in! And everybody*
> *who's already in, Out with you, too if*
> *you disapprove! We go everywhere*
> *together, and we do everything*
> *together. If we're not allowed in*
> *together, we just won't fuckin' go. To*
> *hell with you, and your judgment and*
> *intolerance!"*

I cried for the me I had known and for the person I'd become. I cried for the mom and wife my family knew, and for the one they had ended up with. For two nights, I wrote and re-wrote. I threw away pages damp with tears and others crumpled in anger. At times, I meticulously edited each page. Others, I just copied the words over and over again. Finally, when words and tears no longer flowed, I neatly stacked my pages, shoved them in the folder on my desk, and let it be.

Then came the morning of my turn to read aloud, and I too, shook as I read with quivering voice, and I too, cried as I chronicled my relationship with *my* DOC. But as I concluded, I came to realize it was about the process, not the end product. It didn't matter at all what was on my paper, any more than it mattered what anyone in that room thought of it. So I cleared my throat, gutted it up, and finished my reading:

"Alcohol, I'm scared to let you go. You were always there for me. Picked me up when I was feeling down, relaxed me when I felt tense, and made the good times even better. Then you turned on me, and now there are no good times together – ever. But I keep crawling back to you, begging for more, like a sick, pathetic, battered victim.

"You, once the maker of all things better, now the Betrayer. You, who eased my restlessness and took the edge off, have put me on an edge so thin and sharp, now the only way I can stay

balanced and tolerate this excruciating mental, emotional and physical pain is to drink again. And then again, again and again. But we turned a corner, didn't we? The party's been over for a long, long time, and the relief you once gave is now an elusive memory I chased until I was busted up and finally, defeated.

"Yes, I'm scared to let you go. If this is life drinking, I can't bear to think what waits if I stop. I didn't want to keep drinking and seeing the disappointed looks from my children and my husband, but I could not, NOT drink! It's all become a vicious cycle of fearful maintenance that has left me hopeless. Not the kind of hopeless that's declared by an outsider. I am, within myself, for the first time in my life, without hope. Hope that I can manage my drinking, much less, quit completely. Hope that I can stop hurting my beautiful family. Hope for a better, happier life. And hope that I won't be a drunken, sack-of-shit disappointment the remainder of my life. Yeah, that hope's been long-gone.

"But I'm done. You've taken all I'm willing to give you, so go. Haul your ass away from me and my family. Somehow, they haven't given up on me yet, so neither can I."

Did I blow their socks off? Hardly. But the effect on me of honestly putting that history down on paper and then sharing it aloud with the other members of my group was deep and profound. I had written and read truths about myself that I had never even admitted alone, in my bed, in my busy, crazy head. I now trusted each and every one of these people, and they now trusted me. Seventy-two hours before, we'd never even met. And but for this one thing in common, our paths would have never crossed.

When class was dismissed, I grabbed a bottle of water at the Bodega, sat on a bench under a tree and opened some study materials so no one would bother me.

Chapter 9

I was released from SCU and moved into a room after five days. It was good to have semi-private space, but it was mostly satisfying to know that I had reached another milestone in my recovery. The first had been reading my Goodbye Letter, and I only knew that because they announced it in our morning Community Meeting.

"Hey, everybody, Laura read her Goodbye Letter over the weekend, so give up some love to her on that!" And the entire Community turned to me, smiling and shouting congratulations of "Way to go, Laura!" and "Good job!" while those close by hit me with fist bumps and high fives. It had been no kindergarten bullshit at all, and they knew it.

I smiled back and wiped away tears. Lately, it seemed there was always a pool of tears trying to push their way over my lower lids. Sometimes I could fight them off, but most times they were too quick, and I was much too tired and slow. These tears were different though. I felt relief. I felt understood.

* * *

The young lady I moved in with liked Benzos. "Ativan, Xanax, even that crazy-ass Ambien, no preference, really," she said. She was divorced and had two small children. She also had a cell phone hidden under her mattress.

"You're not going to tell on me, are you?"

"I don't see how that would help my Program at all, so no, I'm not telling."

She was nearing her forty-five day mark and was scheduled to be released in a few days. Most of the college-aged people were in Rehab forty-five to sixty days, but older people on Benzos and some other drugs usually stayed in that long too. She had established friendships and spent her spare time playing basketball with the guys in the gym and looking at sober house brochures. She said going to sober living was okay because she wasn't ready to be "out there," a common term for life outside the bubble of Rehab, and one discussed by most with much trepidation. I felt badly that she wasn't able to go home and just be a mom to her kids. I wondered if they would send me to a sober house before I could go home, but I couldn't be bothered with that. Too far down the road to even ponder. I didn't even know how long I was going to be in the bubble.

I felt as if someone had turned up a dimmer switch, pulled open all the curtains, and wiped fog from my glasses. The sky was a bright blue with pure white clouds, and colorful plants lined the sidewalks and overflowed clay pots outside of meeting rooms that were no longer dark and dank, but roomy and bright. The heaviness in my feet was gone, and I no longer had to drag myself from bed.

Chapter 10

"Well, hello to you, this morning!" a female doctor exclaimed when I entered her office. "Just look at you! Welcome back."

"Good morning," I answered.

"I'm Doctor King. I've been out for a few days, so you might not remember me. We met when you checked in."

"Oh, okay. I mean, Yes! I do recognize you now!"

"Well, again, welcome!" she said laughing a bit. "You've come out of the fog a little quicker than I expected."

"I'm sorry, what?"

"Your twinkle is back ... your eyes ... you're bright, present. So, welcome back!"

I felt both proud and embarrassed. "Well, thank you, Doctor. I don't really know what to say to that." I took my seat, and while she reviewed my progress notes on the computer, I tried not to grin as I marveled that my appearance had changed that much. She would certainly know.

*   *   *

Rehab offered transportation to Saturday evening Mass and Sunday morning church to anyone cleared by the medical staff to leave campus. I was freed from SCU and ready to leave campus to check it out. I didn't bring clothes I considered church-worthy, but that was only a fleeting concern. I dressed in the best I'd packed and arrived at the flag pole in the center of campus *on time*, as instructed. Miraculous!

I sat on a bench and took in the morning sunlight. The campus grounds were beautifully maintained. From my bench, two paved pathways led up the hill. One led to the Bodega, the center of campus life. Our student union, if you will. The other, to the right of it, led up to the Newcomers area and the Butt Hut, a gazebo that served as our designated smoking area. Each sidewalk carved a tight, neat path through thick grass and flower beds lush with green plantings and flowering plants underneath blooming crepe myrtle trees. The two opposite paths lead down the hill to the medical area behind me and the cafeteria down to my right. I felt blessed to be sitting in this oasis in the middle of a burned-out Texas summer.

Others waiting for the van stood in small groups talking and laughing. Some looked familiar, but I didn't know a single one. I didn't even know how far we would travel to the church. I imagined this must be what life is like for a small child, people always lining you up, taking you to unknown destinations with very little explanation. But in my new home I questioned very little and just got on with it. They were all still chatting when the van pulled up, so I dug in my purse for a mint, stalling for everyone else to climb aboard.

"Mornin'," the driver said grabbing a clipboard off the dash. "Please sign in and pass it back."

I get it. Insurance. Younger people going MIA to make out while claiming to be at church. Whatever. I signed in, passed the clipboard back and looked around for a seat.

"You *know*, Laura S.," an older guy near the back of the van said. "You don't ever have to sign your full name in here." And there I was, standing alone in front of a bunch of strangers who had stopped everything to stare at the new girl. I surveyed the group.

"Trust me," I said. "Signing my full name ... to get on a van ... to go to church ... while in Rehab, is the least embarrassing thing I've done in a good long while." Laughter filled the van, and I felt relieved.

"Come sit by me, crazy lady. You're my kind of gal, Laura S." A dark-haired woman about my age slid over next to the window and patted the seat next to her. "I'm Kat-with-a-K. It's good to meet you," she said, extending her hand.

We shook hands and introduced ourselves in the usual Rehab manner. She was a drinker too. Our kids were about the same age, and we talked – well, she talked – the entire time the van made its way down the winding road to church. While Kat-with-a-K chattered on, I stared out the window and tried to buck up in spite of the strange situation. The winding road took us past large, beautiful homes set back from the road and boxed in by beautiful white railed fences, and then further out, the road straightened and cut through miles of baked pasture land. I saw we were approaching the church. There was a split-rail fence around a pasture and a white gravel road leading up to its tan brick building. The red, green and blue stained-glass windows were the only color in the middle of that parched field. Our van turned onto the gravel drive, and suddenly I had a knot in my gut.

We pulled into the parking lot, and I watched as mothers held the tiny hands of their wriggling children, hopping and skipping their way to big church. An elderly man was holding his wife's purse as she rocked slowly getting momentum to pull up out of their car. All so normal, yet surreal.

Oh, God. Really didn't think this through. What will they think of us? I'm not up for pity or ridicule. Maybe we'll stay in the van until everyone else is inside. Maybe they won't know I came with these people. This takes the awkwardness and anxiety of visiting a new church to a whole new level! I really should have thought this through. Forget it. The Big Guy knows exactly where I'm visiting from, so nothing else should really matter. I stepped out of the van, took a deep breath and got on with it.

And that was as long as I felt uncomfortable or even cared. The church building was beautiful with arched, stained-glass windows and intricate, dark woodwork and railing surrounding the pulpit. The sanctuary was packed, and the congregation was already on their feet singing. "Love, Divine, all loves excelling// Joy of heaven, to earth come down// Fix in us Thy humble dwelling// All Thy faithful mercies crown." Kat-with-a-K and I quickly spotted room for two, apologized our way down into a pew, and grabbed a hymnal. I found much comfort in the service and the hymns. Everyone sang big and loud, and they often looked at each other and smiled. The preacher was dressed in blue jeans and a starched white pearl-snap shirt, and his message on God's unending grace was for me, and me alone.

And the church? Oh, they knew we were there, and they knew we were from the rehab down the road. But they didn't gawk and whisper, and they didn't shake their heads with pity either. Young and old alike went out of their way to make eye contact and give me a warm smile. After the service, many introduced themselves and thanked me for visiting. They wished God's blessings for me in my Recovery.

I was humbled. I knew if the tables were turned, I would not have been so gracious. That little country church was truly a house of God, filled with His people. God was rockin' and rollin' in my life, and I knew it. There were miracles all around and inside me in my Rehab campus in the hills. And now these people. I was truly blessed that day.

Chapter 11

Joe C. was a pretty big guy, probably six foot two, two hundred fifty pounds, and I liked him from the first day I saw him on campus. He was in charge of the AA Step Study Lectures for those in the early work of their Program, and like all of our AA instructors, Joe was in Recovery himself. "I'm an alcoholic," he said. "I do love cocaine, but only because it keeps that drinking party rocking all night and longer." He was an intense speaker, and everyone really enjoyed his lectures in spite of the fact that he was in the repetition business. It was Joe's job to take newcomers and pound us into admission. Stop with the denial and admit to the reality of your addiction! Joe was all about reality.

"You see this?" Joe was getting started at the front of the Bodega.

When I first arrived, when the nurse from SCU shooed me out of her golf cart into a meeting, the interior of the Bodega was sad and dark to me, like a musty cabin opened up for the first summer stay. But now that I had emerged from the fog of detox and was free from alcohol for the first time in probably twelve years, I found the building to be open and bright and almost always bustling. One entire side was lined with floor-to-ceiling windows looking out onto the patio and the beautifully landscaped grounds then further out into the Hill Country. The opposite side was wood paneled with a large stone fireplace. A big screen TV, podium and large whiteboards lined the front wall.

The kitchenette in the back corner was always stocked with granola bars, nuts, candy, fresh fruit, water and coffee. The kitchen was bustling before meetings as people moved in and out, some discussing serious matters of Recovery in small groups, others joking around and still others bitching and moaning on the periphery. I did my best to keep them there because they were toxic to my Recovery. To be honest, their all-knowing, condescending attitudes reminded me of a part of myself I was trying to separate from.

If an outsider were to walk into the Bodega with no prior knowledge, it would look like a casual cocktail party with some small groups laughing and cutting up while others quietly shared more serious topics of discussion. However, here, there were no cocktails, and our serious discussions were those of Recovery.

"You see *this*!" Joe repeated. He drew a target on a whiteboard.

Everyone quickly settled into their seats, and an aide got up and closed the kitchen door. Down to business.

He tapped his marker on the bull's eye. "Remember when you could hit this every time?" he shouted. "You remember when drinking and using were still fun?" He started pacing back and forth in large strides across the front of the room. He looked like a football coach, waving his arms and coaxing his team to get on board. "You with me? You know, you go out with your buddies, get a good buzz going, have a good time. Remember that?"

Oh I remembered, all right. But it had been a long, long time ago. I gazed out into the hillsides. We did have some good times, my booze and me. What a strange, bittersweet feeling that was. Like reflecting on a recently lost old friend, not truly grasping the finality of it all, holding some hope that there had been a mistake and my friend could come calling again. *Maybe after I take this break. Maybe then I'll be able to drink like a lady.*

Tap, tap, tap, tap! "Now look at you!" Joe frantically banged the marker all over the outer edges of the whiteboard. "Just look at you! You're all over the damn place! Hit the bull's eye? Hell, you can't even hit the target anymore!"

There was some slight laughter, but most of us just stared back at Joe. I sat up straight and leaned forward, as if to hear even better.

"So, you drink some more. Still not *there*!" He pointed to the bull's eye. "Some of you use some more. Nope, not feeling that good feeling yet. So let's go some more, you say. Drink a few more? Still no better. Maybe you snort a few lines? Still can't get *there*!" He banged the bull's eye again. "You just can't get right anymore, can you?" Most everyone in the room was nodding in agreement. I was dumbfounded.

"And guess what? You won't! 'Cause you *can't!* You can't hit this again!" he shouted, banging his marker in the center of the bull's eye. "You kept drinking and using, but you never hit that sweet spot, did you? You know why? Because you *can't!* And don't fool yourself thinking you can come in here and get cleaned up, get some people off your ass and then go back out, start using again and everything will be great. That it will be like the good old days when you got a happy buzz then were able to stop whenever you wanted. Nope! You've got to know those days are gone, people! Your drug of choice, your D.O.C., your using – drugs, drinking, whatever the case – it's crossed an imaginary line, and you can't choose to jump back over it where things were good. You can't erase it, either.

"Don't you agree you would have already done that if you could?"

Most of us reluctantly nodded our heads.

"Show of hands," Joe said, walking down the center aisle. "How many of you guys have told your families, your wives/husbands, parents whomever, that you would quit this time for good?"

Practically every hand raised.

"Uh huh. And how many times have you said that?"

There were varying responses from, "Can't count that high . . . anymore!" to shameful, lowered heads, nodding in agreement. Joe went on.

"And I know you meant it, too. Your families might not know you meant it, but I do, because I did the same thing myself. Oh, I meant it when I said I was going to quit, moderate, whatever. I just *couldn't*. That's not going to change for you, and you've got to accept it.

"Any idea you have that you can ever drink or use again, must be *smashed*!" He slammed his marker down like a gavel. "It's over," he said. And then he stopped. And every one and every thing stopped.

This was a revelation to me! I couldn't remember the last time drinking was fun for me. I just drank. There was no real expectation. I just did it because that's what I do, or so I thought. But the truth is, there *was* expectation, and when alcohol quit working, I drank more. And then more. Some knew they were chasing a feeling, but for me, it was a never-ending cycle I couldn't comprehend or stop. Drinking became as natural and involuntary as breathing, and then it became every bit as necessary.

It was heart-wrenching to accept that this once determined, passionate force had been reduced to such a pathetic, submissive shadow. I was no different than a wino digging through trash for one more sip, and now I understood his prideless pursuit. *Just one more, and I should be good.* But what a relief too, for someone to get in my head and translate the bewilderment I felt in the last days of my drinking. The not knowing how I got from one sip to eight drinks, and then drunk. It would have been impossible for me to talk to anyone about it, even if I had wanted to, because it was inexplicable to me. I couldn't even describe the bewilderment I experienced in the last days of my drinking. Joe knew. And the people sitting around me knew. I saw them shaking their heads in agreement.

As for the uneasiness between drinking? I honestly had convinced myself it was menopause. I thought every woman my age was shaking on the inside and depressed as hell. Some might have been coping better, but all us forty-something women were crawling beneath our skin, right? It was the life cycle, and I was trying to deal with it as best I could, right? Wrong. It was just life, and I wasn't dealing with it at all.

We had a break, and everyone moved outdoors. Any conversation taking place in the Butt Hut was low and serious. Others talked quietly at the picnic tables, and still others just lay on benches staring at the sky. Joe's lecture had hit home and hit hard, and not just for me.

See, addiction does not discriminate. Oh, you could tell who came from big money, who was middle or upper-middle class and those who were living with a lot less who could afford Rehab only because they had a decent job with good insurance. But not one of us was more sick than the other. We'd had good parents and bad parents. The battered, abused and abandoned were no more sick in their addictions than the pampered and privileged. Any country club fat cat who had turned his retirement into a blur of good Scotch and bad golf was as big a mess as the laborer doing meth after a hard-day's work. There were cocky company executives, young entrepreneurs, self-loathing school teachers, bored housewives and just plain old secretaries like me.

Our common denominator was our inability to control the very thing that used to get us right. Once upon a time, we'd found something – alcohol, pills, cocaine, didn't matter – that took the edge off and allowed us to live in our own skin. We assumed everyone felt dissatisfied, fidgety and fretful most of the time, so we never gave much thought to our motive or the pay-off for using. We just did it because it worked so well.

It is possible for some to drink alcohol, pop a Xanax or even snort a few lines of cocaine recreationally, but not for us. We're just wired differently. So somewhere along the way, our DOC didn't just stop working – it turned on us, demanding to run the show, ever-present in every scene. But for us, to not use meant crawling-out-of-our-skin madness. We were sure of it, and we were terrified of it. We were sure of it because we were already experiencing the intense uneasiness, lack of focus, and inexplicable panic. We were terrified because the madness was already seeping in causing a lightning storm of thoughts, emotions, regrets and remorse. If this was life using, we were certain we could not bear what surely awaited us if we were to stop.

Chapter 12

Melissa moved in with me as soon as she arrived. She was a twenty-eight year-old divorced mother of two from a Dallas suburb. She didn't have to admit through SCU because she had detoxed at home, but within the first couple of days, she had fallen off the grid. She wasn't in meetings, and she didn't stop by our room on breaks. A staff member said she was down in SCU. She wasn't done with detox after all. Even though her DOC was meth, something I knew nothing about, I had volunteered to be her mentor because she was my roommate.

She bounced in and out of SCU three times her first week, and I would visit her on my breaks. Her fair, freckled face was almost gray, and I could actually see large individual beads of sweat on her forehead and upper lip. I would wipe vomit off her chin, get fresh cold washcloths for her head and fetch ice chips. Her hands shook so violently, she could hardly get the ice chips in her mouth. There were plenty of nurses to care for her, of course, but I had learned quickly that we took care of each other in our Community. Anyone who had gone before me always reached back to pull me along, and I, in turn, was reaching back to help along another.

"I mean, I did it right that last time I used, I know that," Melissa said one morning as I was digging in her bag for a clean shirt. "I was tweaking hard!"

Tweaking? I'll ask later.

"But I've been puking for weeks! I don't know how much more of this shit I can take!"

"We've all got our different shit to get through," I said, pulling her soiled shirt over her head. "You'll make it. It's just going to suck for a while. You're almost there, and then you get to be my roomie! You are so lucky. It'll be worth it."

She laughed and said she feared she'd never feel good enough to work her Program. "I hope they won't just send me home because I've run out of time, puking and shit. I'm not even close to getting well in here," she said pointing to her head. She eventually spent about twelve hours in the local hospital on an IV. I was grateful I hadn't endured her withdrawal.

Melissa did eventually move in to stay, and we made good roommates. She was young and a little rough around the edges, but I liked her. The meth thing scared me a little bit. *What a white-trash DOC.* But I kept my thoughts to myself.

I usually got to our room after our evening AA meeting around nine o'clock. There was always homework, phone calls to the family, and then prayer, meditation, and a shower. There was always a shower pending for me, no matter the time of day. The temperature was passing the hundred degree mark every blistering day, and it never rained again after my first day there. "I don't know how you Texans bear it! Ya can't even git cowld watah outaya tap down heya!" one of my friends from the North cried. "Trust me," I said. "It's even kicking our asses this summer." So I showered at night, in the morning and again in the middle of the day. Everyone else was hot and sweaty too, so I figured I was tolerable.

One of the first nights Melissa was back in the room, we had both showered and each sat quietly on our beds studying and writing our individual assignments. I called to check my voicemail, and Alli had left a message.

"Hey, Mom, it's Alli. Well ... I love you! I know you're doing good, and I was just thinking about you and wanting to talk to ya, so call when you can! I love you, Mom!" My heart smiled, and my eyes filled with grateful tears.

"Melissa, will it bother you if I talk to Alli while you're studying?"

"Not at all! I talked to my kids earlier."

I pulled out my journal, flipped the pages to find my calling card and my security code info. Tedious, but you get used to it. I called my Alli.

"Mom! You sound great!"

"What do you mean?"

"You just sound so different! Are you feeling as great as you sound? This is fantastic!"

"Wow! I do feel good. I feel so much better. I didn't even know how bad I'd felt! They're really good at what they do here and very kind. So, yes, I am feeling great. Thanks for that, Alli. I needed it!"

We chatted a bit more, and as we wrapped up our phone conversation, I heard a tick, tick ticking sound. It was a sharp tick, like someone picking at their nails. I sneaked a peek at Melissa over my glasses. She was sitting cross-legged with her back to me.

Tick, tick, tick.

What is that?

I hung up the phone.

Tick, tick, tick, it continued.

Is she picking her feet? No, her feet are hanging off the far side of the bed now.

Tick, tick, tick. Now it was becoming like dripping water. I couldn't think of anything else!

Tick, tick, tick.

Is she out of her mind? Is she masturbating right here with me in the room? What will I do if she goes off crazy in here? What do meth heads do when they're losing it? What have I gotten myself into here?

No television to turn up. No ear pods to silence the mystery.

Tick, tick, tick.

I didn't want to be rude and just flat out ask her what the hell she was doing. She was just now well enough to live in a room. Or *was* she? I was kind of scared of her. She was a meth addict, after all. I didn't want to start any crap because I had to live with her.

Tick, tick, tick.

I can't take this anymore!

I went to the bathroom to wash my face and brush my teeth. There would be running water and cabinets to open and close to give her time to finish whatever the hell she was doing. I took my bag out from under the sink, rattled toiletries as loudly as I could and located my face wash. I lathered up and looked up in the mirror.

How did I get to this place in my life? Here, hundreds and hundreds of miles away from home, living with a meth head and her weird tick, tick, ticking. I'm not like her. I'm a forty-nine year-old wife and mother of three! I wiped off the soap and caught myself in the mirror again. *No. I'm an alcoholic in Rehab. That's all I really am.*

I sat on the toilet, laid my head on the sink counter and let the tears flow. I cried quietly though, because I didn't want any conversation whatsoever. Not about the crying, the damn ticking, my meth-mate, none of it.

How can I feel so alone when I spent all day in a group like some child? What will be left of me after all the tearing down is done? Who will I even really be without my drink?

Chapter 13

The morning after the ticking episode, I was still freaking out about my meth-mate, but it wasn't something I wanted to discuss with anyone. Our Community was good about keeping judgments and gossip to a minimum, and I didn't want anyone whispering about my roommate. Besides, who knows what I might be doing that she finds freakishly weird. She was stuck with an old lady for a roommate after all. So, in my quest for silence, I sat with Elise at breakfast. She didn't always feel the need to fill the air with words like some did.

Elise was in her mid-sixties and looked European with her long face, light thin hair and large, bad teeth. I found her odd when we met in SCU. "Greetings! I am pleased to meet you, but for our mutual circumstance." She disgusted me, shuffling along with her stiff legs and strangely protruding belly, framed by long, otherwise boney extremities, and her white, flat ass glowing at night as she changed clothes without closing her curtains. She terrified me, exposing me to myself as I trudged along with my heavy legs and ever-narrowing frame. Pitiful. Frightening.

But now she had become my friend, and I knew her to be honest, quirky and kind.

"Good morning, Laura!" She smiled big as she stirred her coffee.

"Morning, Elise!" She was sitting at a perfect table for only two by the windows.

"I decided to sit here by the windows today," she said gazing outside. "I thought seeing some of our woodland creature friends would be a lovely way to start the day."

"That would be nice."

Our cafeteria jutted out of a large hill, and windows around half the room provided a beautiful panoramic view of a valley and the hills on the other side. Deer would come right up beside the windows and feed on the small trees and grass, grateful for our little oasis in the middle of their dried out hillsides. I remembered it being simply noteworthy at first. Now I appreciated their visits for the beautiful treat they actually were.

I set my tray down across from Elise and left to get some juice. I had decided not to have orange juice while I was in Rehab. The jury was still out, but I was afraid the OJ might serve as a trigger. I couldn't remember having orange juice without vodka. Some believed in triggers, others explained it like this: *If something is a trigger for you, tough shit! You need to get spiritually fit! The real world goes on, whether you're sober or not. You can drive four blocks out of your way to avoid your old liquor store, but there will be another one around the next corner. You can avoid your old drug hood, but someone else will be around to hook you up another day. Triggers are bullshit.*

My personal recovery goal was to be able to go anywhere I wanted in my sobriety. Clubs, bars, parties, any and all of it. I just didn't want to know if orange juice was a trigger right now. I was amazed I hadn't craved a drink one time since my arrival, even after being taken off detox meds. I wasn't ready to test the trigger theories yet. Apple juice was the only available juice I hadn't spiked with vodka, so apple juice it was.

We buttered our toast and seasoned our eggs in welcomed silence. Elise had recently earned some street cred among the ladies now, especially the collegiate women.

"Those women you're talking about," she said in our women's AA group one night. "Those who screwed your husbands or your boyfriends? That was me. I was promiscuous. Well, hell, we are to be honest, are we not? I was a slut."

"Elise!" the young women squealed and giggled like girls at a sleep over. Then they sat up straight, not wanting to miss a single juicy morsel of this surprise.

"Indeed. And it's not something I'm proud of. I started drinking when I was thirteen, and I started betraying friendships and screwing boys all at the same time."

Deep down, you knew someone was putting out back in the day; nevertheless, it came as a shock to us all. If there had been a Least Likely to Whore Around Award, Elise would have nabbed it prior to that meeting. But the nervous truth-or-dare-type giggling soon subsided as Elise's eyes filled with tears telling of her promiscuity, betrayal and most of all, her horrible, deep shame in it all.

"I can't blame the drinking completely, but it certainly paved the way for making some poor choices. Now sober, I can see that the slutty behavior and the shame afterward have been something I've been drinking my way through ever since. As I told Laura when I came in, I would tidy up the house after my husband left for work, and when the music for my soap opera began at two o'clock, it was time for wine, and once it was time for wine, there was no longer time for anything else. Soap song, wine, and then nothing else the remainder of the day," she said, shaking her head.

"During her soap?" Theresa whispered to me. "Mine started with Good Morning America!"

I had pictured Elise as a classy drunk. She would have her brie and fancy crackers laid out on fine China. She would begin with an expensive bottle of wine, poured into a beautiful crystal wine glass. But she assured me I need not be impressed with her wine drinking, as it was a sloppy, sloppy affair that completely disgusted her husband, and now that she was sober, filled her with shame.

We briefly discussed our upcoming schedules over breakfast and then parted ways to brush our teeth, large and small, respectively, and get on with our busy day.

*   *   *

Melissa was in our room when I returned, and before the door even closed behind me, she said, "I pick at myself, usually my legs." She pulled up her pant leg to reveal hundreds of small, round sores. "It's a meth thing, just so you know. Don't even know I'm doing it."

What the hell am I supposed to say to that?

She walked over to the vanity and started brushing her hair. "See, it's what you do when you're using. Well, there's a lot of stuff you do when you're using meth," she said, gazing out of the window rather than look me in the eye. "You screw ... screw a *lot* ..." Then she laughed awkwardly, as if she were surprised at her own frankness, embarrassed, even. Then her smile quickly disappeared.

"And your boyfriend you're using with? He talks you into doing three-ways with a girl who *was* one of your best friends, and now you can't even stand to look at her anymore. Yeah, did that. And you spend all night watching out the back door for people in your backyard, but only you can see them." She was brushing her hair so hard it had to hurt. "And you ask your kids over and over, 'Can't you see him? He's standing right there by the back fence?' And after they try real hard to see him for a while, they just say, 'No Mama,' and walk off and go play."

Is she gonna breathe?

"But not you," she continued at a manic pace. "You're standing guard because you're a good mom, and you don't want him to move because he might move toward your house, and your babies are in there and ..." Then she suddenly shook herself back to the present and said, "Whoa! Wow! Sorry about that!" and laughed nervously again.

I had been stacking and un-stacking my books and folders from my desk to my bed and then back because the speed of her monologue was creeping me out as much as the content, and I didn't want to make eye contact.

"It's okay," I said, and somehow it really was. She had to talk to someone, right?

"Sorry. Anyway, so I picked at my legs when I was using, and I guess it's just habit now. So, if you see me doing it, just yell, 'Knock it off, Melissa!'"

"Okay, will do."

"I'd like to have my legs clear up while I'm in here. Then I could wear shorts again."

So, that's why she's wearing jeans in this God-awful heat. That must suck.

Melissa started putting on her makeup, and I went to the bathroom.

"Hey!" I yelled from behind the door, "I've got some really good fake tanning lotion if you'd like to borrow it. That might help. I don't know if it will make your sores darker, though."

"Thanks! I'll try it, and if it works, I'll get some when my family comes to visit the first weekend I can leave campus. Thanks a lot, Laura!"

Melissa was still a little rough around the edges, and some of her phone calls got so heated I would leave the room, but we made good roommates. We weren't particularly chatty, but we had a routine that worked for us. She had a different circle of friends during the day, and the only activities we shared were the Community Meetings in the morning and AA in the evenings. At night we studied quietly in our room.

"Knock it off, Melissa."

"Thanks."

My new normal.

Chapter 14

I was so excited Leroy and Matt were coming to see me. It had been weeks since I left home, and although I wasn't homesick, I did need to see Leroy. I really needed Leroy to see me. I was working hard and feeling so much better already. I wanted him to know I was okay. Leroy had been having trouble sleeping since I left. I, on the other hand, was sleeping better than I had in years.

"Baby, you sleeping okay? That's a long time to be away from your own bed," he would say almost every day when we talked on the phone.

"I'm sleeping better than I have in years. Years!"

"Well, ain't that some shit," he'd say laughing. "I'm at home in my own bed, and I'm not sleeping well at all!"

"I don't know what to tell you, because I'm up, rested, with no alarm, at 4:30 or 5:00 every morning!"

"*You?* This *is* messed up!"

That was a fair statement. I was perpetually late – to bed late, up late, arriving late, everywhere, late, late. Before my job at the high school, I always worked as a legal assistant for trial lawyers, notorious for their procrastination and late nights. They would overlook my tardiness, knowing they could parlay that into a late work night.

But I was so excited about their arrival I hardly slept at all the night before, and woke up with giant bags under my eyes and my skin looking old and dry. Like my old self, actually. *This is unacceptable! I feel so much better, and I'm going to look like hell when they arrive.* Feeling like a superficial co-ed calling on a sorority sister for help before a date, I ran down the sidewalk to the One-Oh-One.

The One-Oh-One was just a few doors down from Melissa and me. Their room was no different than ours, but it was transformed into a luxurious suite accessorized with their designer bags, fancy clothes, small appliances and beauty items. I wondered if there was a butler hidden in there somewhere. I tapped on the door.

"Good morning!" Tiffany said as she flung the door wide open. She was in a fluffy white shorty robe that looked like it came off the back of the bathroom door at the Waldorf Astoria. Behind her, designer shoes and clothing littered the floor, curling irons and blow dryers hung over door knobs, and a professional clothes steamer stood in one corner. *I am in the right place!*

"Good morning, ladies," I answered. "I'm so sorry to bother this early, but ..."

"Oh, don't be silly, come on in!" Tiffany hid behind the door, realizing her risk of exposure.

"Good morning, Laura!"

"Good morning, Miss Georgia." I smiled and waved and looked back to Tiffany. Morning Tiffany looked remarkably different than Daytime Tiffany, further confirming I was in the right place.

"What's up, lady?" Tiffany was wiping her face with a wash

cloth that was certainly not Rehab-issued. For a second, I wanted to snatch it and put its cloud-like softness against my face, but I shook myself back to the task at hand.

"Look at my face!" I screeched. "My husband and son are coming today, and I look like hell! Can you help me?"

"Oh, sweetie, you do have some baggage underneath the eyes. C'mon in, dahling. Let me help."

Miss Georgia glided through her morning routine. "I would love to tell you we failed to pick up the place last night, or that this disarray results from getting ready in the morning, but it looks like this all the time. We're just dreadful!" she said. Her sparkling eyes and beautiful smile always made me smile back immediately. She reminded me of a Merle Norman model with her taut beautiful skin and smooth silver hair.

"Oh, Miss Georgia, who cares?" I laughed. "Besides, who is rude enough to visit this early, but me?"

"Oh, hon, don't you worry about a thing. Tiff will get you some eye cream, and you will return to your beautiful self in time for your husband. Did you not sleep well last night?"

"No, not at all. Think I was too excited. Now, just look at me! It's just that I feel so much better, and I look so bad!"

"No, no, no. Truly, you don't. But yes, the eye luggage must go." She waved it away with her hand high in the air.

Tiffany rattled around in make-up cases and returned with a small pod of cream. "This is from the gods," she said, ceremoniously placing the pod in my palm and closing my fingers around it.

"Oh, indeed," Miss Georgia said. "I use that too, and it is gold, honey. Pure gold."

"But I don't have anything to put it in!"

"Oh, just take it all," Tiffany said, waving away my worries with her diamond-clad hands. "Just take it all and get yourself beautied up for your husband. We'll meet up later."

"You ladies are the best! I knew where to come because y'all always look so beautiful. Thank you so much!"

"Aww, you are so sweet," they said in unison.

"Go ... and be beautiful," Tiffany said with a wink.

"Thanks much again!" I practically ran back to my room to rid myself of my eye luggage with the pod of gold.

Tiffany appeared out of nowhere in our large group one day. She was never on the board in our Community Meeting as a newcomer needing a mentor, and none of the other newcomers recalled seeing her in their first meetings. There were some whispers that she had been allowed to detox in a private suite, but nobody could tell you where that might be. She did drip money, so as usual, the claws came out from some of the ladies when she appeared because she was so beautiful and, as I said, she dripped money. But even the harshest women couldn't resent Tiffany for long because she was the sweetest, most gracious lady you'd ever want to meet. She too, was an alcoholic. The rest didn't make any difference to me.

Miss Georgia was in my therapy group. She was all alone in this world, she would say, having lost her husband ten years ago and her only son in a car accident when he was twenty-two. She was also very wealthy – she had staff. Miss Georgia was addicted to OxyContin, thanks to a back injury and a doctor who increased her dosage whenever she complained about aches and pains.

"I thought it was okay," she said with tears in her eyes. "He had been my doctor for years, and I trusted him." Pissed me off.

Her staff took her to another doctor for evaluation when she began spending all her days falling and sleeping, she said. "I thank God they cared to get me here. I had been so active, working out, lunching with my girlfriends, shopping and everything. I thought I couldn't do it anymore because of my back and because I'm just getting old. Come to find out, I'm a damn drug addict! How dreadfully embarrassing!" She was off her old lady scooter, as she called it, in two weeks, and that pleased her greatly.

I admired those two ladies. Their lives weren't in a shambles like most of ours were. They could pay their bills, buy all their DOC they wanted, afford plenty of beautiful clothes – employ staff, even! Yet they came for help just like the rest of us regular folk because their DOC had taken on a life of its own.

I recalled what the Bible says about it being easier to ride a camel through the eye of a needle than for a rich man to get into heaven and decided that's probably true about getting sober too. Ego. Ego. Ego. I wondered if I would have made it to Rehab if other parts of my life weren't falling apart. Maybe I would have continued my unsuccessful intake modifications, such as Drink Wine Only, an abandoned effort because wine no longer took me where I needed to go, or Only Drink after Five O'clock, which I could maintain except on weekends and holidays, but also meant staying up later, because I had to drink myself to a certain point in order to sleep.

*　　*　　*

I could hardly concentrate during our Sunday meeting and found myself staring out the glass walls of the Bodega hoping to see Matt and Leroy. I didn't know how we were to meet up with visitors and never asked. There was a gnawing sense that something might go wrong, and my family time would be denied, so I figured the less said, the better.

I was first out of the Bodega at noon and headed down the hill towards the medical area. If they weren't there, they might be at the administration building where I checked in. But as I was looking down to maneuver the tiny stone steps down the hill, I glanced up and saw my Matt, grinning and watching my every move. I almost tripped as I rushed to give him a big hug, and then Leroy, who had been pacing the parking lot, out of view.

"You're just out ... like walking around and stuff? I mean, I don't know what I'm trying to say ... it's just nice here, and you're walking around like ... I'm sorry, I don't know what I mean," Matt said.

"Oh no!" I grabbed his hands. "You thought I was locked in a cinder block room? Oh my God, I'm so sorry!"

"Well, yeah, kinda," Leroy said. "You know, Alli never saw your room, and those are the only kind of places I've ever seen!"

"I feel terrible I've worried y'all so much! I assumed you'd Google it after I told you where I was going. I mean, good grief, Matt, you guys Google everything! What the hell?"

He laughed and turned red. "Well, that's true, so I don't really have an excuse, do I?"

"I can leave campus. Let's grab some lunch."

We had an excellent lunch and an awkward visit. I was thrilled to see them and more thrilled for them to see I was doing great, but the strain with my own family was just too much. We small-talked through our chicken-fried steaks and potatoes, with Matt saying every few minutes, "Mom, you look so great!" We returned to campus and checked in with Mr. Lucas in the guard shack.

"Laura, don't forget to stop by medical and test in!"

"Got it! Thanks!" As we pulled past the gate, I looked up from digging in my purse and said, "I have to be drug and alcohol tested if I leave campus without staff. Won't take but a minute. No big deal." But I had forgotten that my new normal wasn't their normal at all, and as they tried to mask their horror, I could feel it filling the spaces between us. "Seriously, guys, no big deal at all. Be back in a jif." I jumped out as soon as we parked and headed for the medical building.

I briefly felt shame – my son was there for God's sake! But shame no longer gripped me, so I pushed it aside and got on with my testing. I entered the SCU to find Miss Verna on duty. Excellent. "I had lunch with the family," I said in my best Godfather voice. "Word on the street is, you got sumthin' to sayabowtit. You got a problem?"

"Pee in the cup, leave it in the bathroom. I'll get you back to your family as quick as I can, you smart a—aleck."

"That's a nice save there, Miss Verna! I love you." She grunted her response. God, I loved her cranky ass.

Matt and Leroy stood waiting in the parking lot, and I wondered which one of them broke their awkward man-silence with a "Well, that was weird" while I was inside. *Give them a break, who knows what to say when their mom or wife is on leave from rehab?* We walked to the center of campus and stood while I pointed out my room and the buildings where I attended classes.

"What's going on over there?" Matt asked, pointing to a large group of people.

"Oh, that's the Butt Hut, designated smoking area. Ninety percent of us smoke; you'd think they could make it larger." My Community passed us as we stood talking – young and old, tatted up goth, and buttoned-down preppy. *This has to be mind-blowing for them. I'm suddenly so uncomfortable!*

"Well, I've got classes, and you two have a long drive so ..."

"Oh yeah, we best get going," Leroy said. "You do look great, and I'm glad you're doing so good."

"You do, Mom. It's amazing!"

"Thank you for saying that! I am much better. Leroy, I don't want you to come down again until it's time for me to leave. It's too far, and it won't be long before I'm out anyway."

"I'm not sure I like that, but ..."

"Look, I've got a lot of work to finish before they'll let me leave. That's what I do on weekends, so I will work hard, and then I'll be ready for you to take me home! Okay?"

"Do they give you a date to check out ... leave, or be dismissed?"

"Nope. Not yet."

He agreed to hold off on the visits, and we all hugged and kissed our goodbyes. I fully expected to feel homesick sad when they left, but I didn't. This melting pot world of alcoholics and addicts understood me, they were my recovery family. I had no desire for the two worlds to collide again.

Chapter 15

I could tell it was going to be a good day because the energy on campus was like that of a game day, when people of totally different backgrounds, occupations and beliefs come together with one thing in common, and the bond is strong. Every day began with a Community Meeting at eight o'clock. Yep, a bunch of drunks and addicts were up, dressed and had even had a full breakfast by 8:00 a.m. Miraculous! The Community Meeting in the Bodega began with a moment of silence for the alcoholic and addict still suffering and announcements from staff members about scheduling changes. Then the Community would sing "Hit the Road, Jack" as we waved the counselors and other staff members out of the room. The inmates ruled the asylum for thirty minutes.

Each week different members were nominated to lead the group, and they brought us our morning news. Weather, hot as hell, still no rain. Business news, gas prices up, stocks down. And snippets of pop culture, Amy Winehouse finally did herself in. Not a light subject in Rehab.

Other members announced the names of newcomers who were still detoxing in SCU, and someone of like age and usually the same drug of choice, would volunteer to check on them in SCU and mentor them in their first few days. Newcomers attending their first Community Meeting were given an initiation of sorts that ended with a presentation of a handful of pocket change. "And here's some cents to borrow for the sense that you lack. When you do the work and find your own, you can give it back." It was a silly and fun way to start the day. I watched staffers outside shaking their heads and smiling as our laughter spilled out onto the sidewalks.

Praises and Gratefuls were solicited from the crowd each morning, as well. People would raise their hands and recognize someone who had helped them through a particularly difficult day or with one of the Twelve Steps in their Recovery, and after each, the group responded with a collective, "Way to step up!" If God was surely the only one who could have helped, as He very often was, that person acknowledged God's help, and the group responded, "Way to go, God!" This was good spiritual bull for the entire group. And every single morning, when he was sure all other Gratefuls were complete, Bill C. stood before the group and made his own grateful declaration.

Bill C. was a good-looking forty-something guy, shaved bald with a black mustache and goatee. He obviously worked out and carried himself with an air of confidence bordering on cockiness. He was soft-spoken and reserved, usually standing quietly on the periphery with one or two other men during our breaks while the rest of us chain-smoked in the Butt Hut. Occasionally, he would find it necessary to gently brush off flirtatious overtures from the younger women. But Bill, we discovered, was a passionate protector of the underdog, and he had taken Manny under his wing one day after another member, edgy from detox, had snapped at Manny in a meeting, breaking his tender heart. And as the crushed Manny rushed from the Bodega, Bill ran to his side, put his arm around him and eventually sat and talked with him on the patio while we all watched from inside. It was something to see that big, strong, quiet guy in his tender moment with that young man. When Bill returned from the patio, he respectfully requested the floor and very convincingly assured us no further disrespect of Manny would be tolerated because, he said, "Well ... because I love that little fucker!" And so now Bill stood before us each and every morning and boisterously made his grateful declaration, as if he were our king.

"And I ..." Bill would say, with his chin pointed towards the ceiling and his arms outstretched towards his subjects. "I am grateful for Manny ... because?"

"Because we love that little fucker!" we shouted in unison.

And Manny, sitting cross-legged in his chair, usually picking at his bare feet or braiding a small section of his hair, would smile like the little boy he was deep inside, rather than the twenty-something year-old man he actually was, and those nearby would pat him on the shoulder or tussle his long, unkempt hair. Manny, we decided, was a beautiful, sweet soul born a couple of generations too late. He would skinny dip in the pool late at night and claim he had bathed. He would stash granola bars from the Bodega in his shorts and rarely show for meals. He would sputter and stutter in meetings and make the most innocent, decent, and profound observations. Manny was our village idiot. Manny was fried.

After Bill's initial declaration, everyone in the Community looked out for Manny until suddenly one day, he was gone. We later learned his parents had taken him to another facility with "more structure." Someone saw his parents while they were on campus to gather their boy and reported the following: "They were as fuckin' buttoned-down as Manny was loose." Go figure. Even after he was gone, the Community continued to profess its love for that little fucker each and every morning.

After our great Community Meeting, everyone was smiling more than usual as we passed each other on the sidewalks, each heading to our group or individual therapy sessions, Twelve Step Study or physical activities. The AA Twelve Step instructors led the largest meetings of the day, and they were picking up on the positive energy emanating from ninety-plus alcoholics and addicts in one room, and they were on fire with their teachings. The staffers who made sure we put out our cigarettes and got to class on time were smiling and nodding at each other as we teased them in their prodding. "I'm going, Miss Leeza. I know, I know. Nobody wants an alcoholic who can't make it to work on time!"

Viv, my favorite aide, said to me, "Miss Laura, I see you found your smile! Keep it, Hon. It suits ya." I didn't even know I'd lost it. We fist bumped as we passed. That positive energy built on itself throughout the day as people buzzed back and forth between tables in the cafeteria, joking and laughing, and spirited discussions and debates erupted at picnic tables, in the Butt Hut and across the grounds.

118

Our final meeting each day was a campus-wide AA Meeting in the Bodega. Eight o'clock, mandatory. Harrison and Paul were leading, and they were always full of fun. Paul was a tall, thin redhead advertising guy from Pennsylvania. He couldn't leave the K-2 alone. "It's the crack of weed, man. High, high, high, then gone way too quickly." Harrison was a short, chubby guy in his forties, and he and his wife owned a wine and cigar bar. *Nirvana!* Very early in my stay, I struck up a conversation with him at the Butt Hut when I asked him what kind of fancy cigarettes he was smoking. Dunhills. During that conversation, he said, "Now hold on just a minute. I'm not saying I'm all-in. I'm here to find out if I have a problem. I'm not saying I'm ... well, you know ... *alcoholic.* I'm here to listen and learn about all this." It really pissed me off because I had opened up to him, but I didn't have to say anything because Rachel walked between us.

"*Right,*" she said rolling her eyes at Harrison. "You hold tight to that, big guy." She lit the Marlboro Red hanging from the side of her mouth, plopped on a bench, crossed her skinny legs and began blowing smoke rings, looking bored. Rachel's drug of choice was "Whatever the fuck *you're* carrying," she said.

Rachel's coal black hair was shiny with gel and pulled up in short, pointy spikes shooting in different directions from her head. She wore black eye shadow, and her thick, black eyelashes were barely parted top to bottom, like she was still high. Her full lips were exaggerated with black liner around deep purple lipstick. She wore black tank tops revealing, what one could only hope, were the majority of her scary tattoos. But for her painted face and body,

Rachel was pasty white and frighteningly thin. Her worn jeans hung on her protruding pelvic bones with the help of a thick, black belt with silver studs. Such was Rachel's attire, day in and day out, the predictable uniform of the supposed edgy non-conformist.

She sat in front of me one time in the Bodega, tramp stamp rising out of the back of her jeans. That was no big deal, practically all the young girls had them and were all too eager to show them off. But that day Rachel plopped in front of me – that's when I saw it. The secret hidden beneath her over-produced darkness. Just to the right of her winged tramp stamp, barely peeking over her biker-chick belt. Tweety Bird! *Tweety Bird*, for God's sake! She quickly hitched up her pants on each hip after she sat down, but he had already revealed himself to me. He all but winked at me as he descended below her belt line, leaving only the larger, scarier wings fluttering up from her butt crack. I didn't say a word because Rachel didn't take any shit from any body. I knew that because she said it all the time.

But now Harrison, once a self-declared observer who never contributed to any AA Meetings, was leading one on the topic of "Acceptance and Gratitude."

In our AA Meetings you didn't wait for someone to call on you. There might be two or three seconds of silence after someone spoke, and then someone else would offer in, "I'm so-and-so, and I'm an alcoholic" or, "I'm an addict."

It was rapid fire that evening. Practically everyone was engaged, and the topic was perfect for the high-energy, positive day we'd been having. I dove in. It was my first time to speak in a meeting.

"Hi, I'm Laura, and I'm an alcoholic." Pause for the response.

"I know I don't know very much about my disease. I've certainly realized that much since I got here." *Crap, my voice is quivering.* "But what I do know is that I'm grateful I'm here. My drinking was ... well, my drinking got to the point where it was like riding on a train that was going really, really fast. It was just so damn fast ..." My voice was trailing off almost to a whisper. My face was hot, my chest was pounding, and I was short of breath, but I pressed on.

"I was on it– the train–and I couldn't figure how to get off. Too scared to just jump off. Too ashamed to ask someone how to slow it down or pull me off. I was just stuck. I was so scared. So ... I drank ... some more. After I'd had a few drinks, the panic would ease, and then after a few more, all the panic was gone, and I just really didn't give a shit." When I looked up, most of the Community was turned toward me, nodding in agreement with gentle sympathetic eyes. Others sat with heads lowered almost to their knees, staring at their own wringing hands or their tapping feet. Then the sympathetic eyes stopped blinking and the feet stopped tapping. It was as if time had stopped.

When I was little, and forced by my grandmother to perform on stage at piano recitals, I would get what I called The Swoosh when it was my turn to take the stage. Everything in my periph went to a blur, and the only sounds I could hear were that of my own feet on the wooden steps to the stage and their echo in the back of the large auditorium.

As I looked around the room, blurred around the edges with the gray of my early days creeping back in, my breath shortened and my legs went to Jell-O. My words were coming from some unknown place, describing feelings never conscious to me before. Mystified as to why I was suddenly able to articulate the feelings and further, that I had even spoken in such a large group in the first place, I slowly picked up my water bottle from beside my chair and sipped. Eyes blinked, feet tapped and I released a heavy sigh. These people were becoming my most trusted allies. They were my family now. On I went.

"I don't know what made me give up and make the call. I honestly don't. I know that pushing the button on that last number on my phone, yeah, that took a while." I held my left hand up as a mock phone and my right index finger just above it, shaking it profusely, and their laughter pushed me on.

"I bet I sat on my bed with my finger over that last number for fifteen minutes. Shit. I had to get plastered to make the call," I said. "That's how messed up I am." I hung my head in shame, expecting groans of disgust or disbelief, or maybe mocking laughter. Heavy silence.

"Just knowing when I pushed that last number, someone was going to answer, and it would be over, that was terrifying. I mean, the train *would* stop. But I also knew the cat would be out of the bag. I would have said it out loud. I would be ... well I guess I would be accountable. It would be on me now. From now forward, it would be on me, and that scared me to death."

I paused for a moment and swallowed hard. My throat was tight. I wiped away a few tears and pushed through.

"Well, actually, I do know why I made that call. It was a God thing, I guess. Had to be because nothing else was different than before. Yeah, it was a God thing, and for that, I'm very grateful. So ... Whew!" I took a deep breath and laughed nervously. "So, now I'm in acceptance that I am an alcoholic, and, it's weird, but I'm grateful for that too. It's a good day. Thanks for listening. That's all I've got."

Quiet thanks came from the people sitting around me. I took another deep breath, grabbed my water bottle again and took a big swallow. I pondered whether or not I should get up and run to the bathroom. My stomach was boiling. *I seriously might crap my pants. I think I best sit tight.*

Another person in The Community introduced himself as an alcoholic/addict and began speaking. "It's been a good day for me too. I'm learning what I need to do to stay sober, and it's starting to click," he said. "Stuff's making sense to me now. It didn't when I first got here, so that's cool. I'm grateful for that. I can accept that I can't drink and use anymore, that I'm different from people out there, and I'm good with it now."

"What the *fuck*?" A young woman's voice screeched out of nowhere.

Whoa! Nobody knew where she was, but we were all leaning around each other and rising slightly out of our seats trying to figure it out. Everyone looked at each other, shaking their heads in confusion. The stranger continued.

"I don't know what y'all are in here for, but this isn't all rainbows and ponies and shit!"

We all recoiled as if someone had dropped a turd in our Happy Cupcake.

"It's Lindy," Kat leaned back and whispered to me.

I shrugged my shoulders because I couldn't remember any woman named Lindy.

"She came in a couple of days ago. Still detoxing."

"Oh," I answered, and continued looking around as the new girl continued shouting.

"This fucking shit is hard! I've already tried this before, and being back in isn't something I can manage to be *grateful* for, I can tell you that. Y'all are all sitting around here with your Kumbaya bullshit. It's just fucked up!"

I could hear mumblings around me of 'Holy crap!' 'What a wet blanket, damn!' and 'Debbie Downer in 'da house.' Caesar, who was sitting next to me, mumbled under his breath, "No, *that's* fucked up. *You're* fucked up." He leaned into my ear and continued, "I don't have to listen to her shit. Who is that, anyway?"

"Lindy," I whispered. "She's new. Detoxing."

"Oh." Caesar sat back in his seat, stretched out his legs underneath the chair in front of him and shook his head.

After perusing the room a bit, I finally got an eye on her. She was a tall blonde, sitting on the second row. I was in my usual position, fourth row from the back. Her head was down in her hands now, elbows on her knees.

The aide who sits in the back to make sure we all sign in

124

and don't skip out of the meeting is also supposed to make sure we maintain AA Meeting decorum. But she simply shifted her big, fat butt in her chair and said nothing. Then there was a big, fat pregnant pause in the room.

"Okay! Well, I'm Joy, and I'm most definitely an alcoholic!"

"Hi, Joy," we answered. She continued, and The Community was grateful for the tension-breaker that was Joy.

In a room full of addicts and alcoholics, self-centered by definition, there was an amazing amount of patience and understanding. We all had been in our own meltdown place. Maybe it was before we even got to Rehab, when we were giving up and giving in. Or it might have been when we first arrived. Some people didn't get to their meltdown place until they were weeks into their treatment, when the reality and finality of sobriety soaked in and overwhelmed them. When you're in your disease, emotions are stuffed down, soaked in booze, pushed through veins or absorbed by pills. When you're detoxing, they find their way to the surface. Sometimes they bubble up. Sometimes they rush in like waves.

Chapter 16

On a break between AA Big Book studies, I plopped down in the Hut and fired one up.

"How's it going, Tabi?"

She was sitting in a corner alone, and when she looked up at me I could see she was crying in silence. She responded by pointing to her puffy, wet face and shrugging her shoulders.

"I'm sorry you're having a bad day. Anything happen, or just a shitty day?"

"I don't know. I just don't know," she said shaking her head and wiping her nose on her hand, then her hand on her shorts.

"I just don't get it. I mean, I don't understand why I can't kick this thing, Miss Laura." Her voice quivered as tears streamed out of her big, brown eyes, and my heart broke as she continued.

"I mean, you don't understand. Like ... I come from a *normal* family. My parents are the best, and I pull this shit? This is the second time I've called them to bring me home ... and ... I just keep fucking things up. It's like I'm watching somebody else do this stuff. Like it's not really me. The stuff that really is me, who I *really am*–where's that stuff?

"I don't mean to sound like I'm bragging or anything, I really don't. I play sports," she paused to wipe her eyes and pull back her long brown hair. Her legs were crossed, and she nervously shook her foot as it dangled in the air.

"I'm an athlete. And ... well, I don't mean this, I don't want you to take this the wrong way, but I'm good, Miss Laura! I'm really good, and ..." Her voice trailed off as she cried softly into her hands.

"Tabitha, I get that. My kids are athletes. I get it. It's what you do. And if you kick ass, well, you kick ass! It's not bragging. Believe me, I get it. Go on." I saw relief as she looked up at me.

"Okay, well, I *do* kick ass. If there's something that has to be done to win, I'm your gal. I step that shit up, you know?"

"Yep. I know exactly what you mean."

"So why can't I kick this thing's ass?" She raised her hands up in frustration, her fingers half-bent and stiff.

"Why can't I beat it? I am so frustrated and confused, and it makes me so mad! It makes me so ... it just makes me so sad, for me and my family." She put her face in her hands, and I could see her shoulders shaking as she cried softly.

"Because we can't kick this thing's ass, Tabitha," I said. "That's how we all ended up here. I'm not saying I've got it all figured out, or that I know everything, because I *don't*. But I know we can't do what we usually do. We can't kick that ass this time. That's why getting the God thing is so important. That's what they're trying to get through to us. We can't, but God, He can."

She raised her head, wiped her eyes and looked at me square for a moment, her big, round brown eyes full of tears, then back at her fidgeting hands.

"Okay. I mean, I know what you're saying. And I was a

127

believer before. I mean I still am. It's not that I don't believe in God or anything like that. I don't know what happened ..." Her voice faded as she wiped her face. Then she cleared her throat and sat upright.

"Thank you. Thanks so much for listening to my bullshit."

"It's not bullshit, and I'll listen to you anytime you want."

The mom in me wanted to hold her tight and whisper that everything was going to be okay, but some of the other Collegiates had made their way into the Butt Hut, and I knew it wouldn't be cool for us to hang out much longer. I put out my cigarette and stepped out onto the sidewalk, squeezing her shoulder as I left.

I marveled at the sheer random madness of it all. Tabitha was beautiful, smart and athletic like my Alli, but Tabitha was here, in Rehab, after living on the streets as a heroin addict.

There was no epiphany. No emotional come-on down-the-center-aisle event. I didn't even pray in the traditional sense I knew. I moved through my day with a conscious awareness that something bigger than I had ever known or experienced was at work. Sometimes God's presence was so palpable it overwhelmed me. At night, my busy, crazy head was quiet, and I rested safe and assured, like a child. I didn't have the clarity to pray most of the time, so I simply sat with God. My desperation had created an openness and willingness to connect with Him, and it was enough. I'm sure of it, because He came and He stayed. What a paradox. Let go, they say. Stop working so hard at life! But to give up that grip, that pushing, crunching, forcing-my-own-will effort was the hardest thing of all for me. Relief from alcoholism is available, they said. Hope can be restored, and joy re-found. "God could and would, if He were sought," AA tells me. I knew He could, He was God, after all. But if He would, that was up for a crazy debate in my head and heart. Had I finally worn Him out with my pleas for help and forgiveness with no change of heart or behavior? Very possibly, I thought, but even if He still would, there was this one strangely daunting caveat. Only if I ask, and then, only if I allow Him after asking. That would be the last delusion of control I would have. Could I do it? I'm a self-reliant, strong woman. Really? Brought to my knees by alcohol, sitting both hopeless and helplessly in Rehab. That self-reliant thing wasn't working out too well for me now. It was exhausting. I was so very tired. Tired of me, tired of drinking, tired of disappointing myself and my family. Tired of fighting for my own will, I would later find out. Early on, I tried to process my days by writing in my journal.

But soon I found writing too often was keeping me from experiencing the moment, causing more reflection than forward movement, so my journal entries became shorter and my quiet time with God became longer. And even amid all the frightening change, for the first time in my life, that quiet time was enough. It was perfectly enough.

Chapter 17

"Those of you still detoxing? I know you've still got a little fuzz floating around in your head, and things aren't real clear right now." Joe was smiling and making swirling gestures over his head, and you knew he understood.

Those who needed it were medically detoxed, and I had been one of them. When I was in it, I thought I was just overwhelmed at the entire situation, but once I made it through detox, I could certainly confirm the lack of clarity.

"Huh? Am I right?" he continued. "It's a little foggy up there, isn't it? That's okay. You're going to be in here with me long enough for the cobwebs to clear and this will start making more sense to you." I put my study materials under my chair and settled back into my seat. Joe paused for people to clear out of the kitchen and take their seats.

"But did it rain? I don't think it's foggy at all today. What's the deal?" It was Fran, or God-Bless-Her Fran, as she existed in my head, an adorable college-aged girl with bobbed blonde hair and a big beautiful smile that rarely left her chubby-cheeked face.

"Fran's about the stupidest life form I've heard speak words," Rachel said to no one in particular as she plopped in a chair in front of Paul and me. Paul leaned towards her. "Hey, not cool. She doesn't need that. We're supposed to be helping each other out.

"I'm not going to be in here long enough to help *that*," she said, rolling her eyes.

Paul gave her a fatherly glare. "Then just don't say a word."

"I've got my own fuckin' problems, man," Rachel said. She turned around, straddled her chair and sat backwards, facing Paul. There were so many thick silver rings on her fingers and studs on her belt clanging around, several others tuned into the conversation.

"Listen," she said. "I don't *hate* the girl, it's just that I can't be taking on anybody else's shit, that's all. First, they say 'be selfish in your sobriety,' then they tell me the answer is to do nice stuff for others. I came in here for myself ... to get better ... and to get some people off my ass."

Fran giggled and turned around. "I hear ya, sister!" She reached for a high five but Rachel left her hanging. She had no clue Rachel had been talking about her.

"I rest my case," Rachel said. Then she turned around and slumped down in her chair facing Joe. I considered her hidden Tweety Bird tat for my personal comic relief.

I could barely tolerate Fran when I first came in. *She's too stupid to speak!* But now I felt sad for her – enabled by her mother to the point of being disabled, and now she was fried.

"You *don't* do laundry?" Taylor asked her one time. "Meaning, what? Because you *won't?*

"Oh, girl no," Fran said. "I don't know *how* to."

"Haven't you ever lived away from home? You're twenty-two years old, for God's sake!"

"I just take it home. My mom's always done my laundry."

"Jesus," Taylor mumbled.

"Who can blame her, if her mom will do it?" Josh said.

Jesse shook his head. "My mom won't take my calls, much less my laundry."

"God!" Taylor said. "Did you bring forty-five days' worth of underwear in here? No, you did not, and that's just gross." And Fried Frannie just laughed and laughed.

Joe continued. "Those of you finished detoxing? You know, you've been in here three, four days or so. Colors are looking brighter, people are making more sense. You know what I'm talking about."

There was soft laughter from some in agreement.

"It's gone!" he shouted.

I jumped.

"It's gone! There's no more in ya! There is no physical craving, so watch the words you use. We talk about the craving in here, but the physical craving is gone for you now. Accept that. Know that. You don't physically need it anymore."

I was stunned! I was relieved.

"So now it's the mental craving, the obsession we talk about in here. And the only thing that can fix that noise in your head, day in and day out, is fixing your spiritual malady. You're an alcoholic," he said pointing in one direction, "And you're an addict," he pointed in another. So you've got a mental obsession about your DOC. You've got to get right here (pointing to his heart) so you can fix that shit up here (pointing to his head). Y'all following me out there?"

Many nodded in agreement, and some just sat still, either confused by the concept or simply still too foggy to even understand the words. Didn't matter. There would be many more opportunities to get it. Joe was all about repetition.

"There you are. You're clean now. Yeah. That's right. That's some news for a room full of people like you. *You're clean!* He pointed in one direction. *You're sober!*" he pointed in another. "But you can still remember it, can't you? Sure you can! Remember how it tastes?" He paused for effect.

"Sure, you do! But that's not all it was for you, is it? No, it was about the planning, the purchase, the mixing ... this is what we're talking about when we talk about the mental obsession. You're not shaking anymore. You don't physically need that drink or that fix. It's gone! But you remember. And there will come a time when you only remember the good stuff. We call that the mental obsession.

"If you're a drinker? You call up your buddies, right? 'Man! It's on tonight, you in?' Or maybe you're just at work thinking about picking up a bottle on your way home. You're doing your little mental game of 'Which liquor store did I go to yesterday or the day before?' Aren't you? Yeah, I know. Because you've gotta mix that shit up so no one knows how much you're really drinking, right? Huh?" He's smiling and laughing and nodding.

Holy crap! Other people do that too?

"But you're so smart you didn't even realize you're drinking so much now that your every other day game, or your every three days in the rotation, whatever game you're playing – it's still a helluva lot of alcohol. Yeah? You with me here?"

Whoa. I'm kind of laughing along, but shit! This is uncanny!

"And you who were out there using? You know what you were doing. It's more than the fix itself, isn't it?"

He took out his phone and started pounding numbers in and put it to his ear.

"No, man! I don't want any of that crap, you know what I like! Meet you when? Yeah, that's cool. You'll hook me up? Cool. Cool."

Laughter.

"But it's already started, hasn't it?"

Silence.

"It's happening already. Your heart rate starts picking up … maybe your mouth starts to water a little bit … you know what I'm talking about." He paused for confirmation from the crowd, and he got it.

"You can feel that needle before you even make it to your dealer, can't you? And you can taste that drink before it's even mixed, can't you?"

And then it happened. I could smell whiskey. Right then and there in the middle of Rehab, I smelled whiskey. I smelled whiskey like whiskey smells when it first splashes over its little ice cube waterfall. I smelled the sweetness and the woodiness of it. I smelled straight up whiskey.

Chapter 18

I was sitting in a corner of the Butt Hut after Joe's lecture when Jesse sat next to me and fired up a smoke. He was a tall, slender young man with a short, tight haircut. He hardly resembled the nervous foot-tapping guy I met in SCU. His face had color, and his eyes, dark and hollow before, were now sparkling blue. He wore small wire-framed glasses and always dressed in pressed buttoned-down short-sleeve shirts. He was a good-looking kid, and I couldn't help but marvel that he was the same age as our oldest. *It could be one of my boys. I mean, look at their mother! Just look at me.* The image of one of our boys being wherever it was that brought Jesse back in here made me both edgy and grateful.

Jesse was sitting on a bench, leaning forward with his arms resting on his legs. He would draw hard on his cigarette and then raise his head to exhale, looking at no one and nothing in particular. I sat cross-legged on the bench beside him, playing with my cigarette on the side of the coffee can someone had decorated in the art room. "There's always hope," it said inside a bright yellow star.

Although I recognized its therapeutic value, I personally didn't spend much time in the arts and crafts room. I just couldn't get the basket-weaving thing out of my mind every time I entered the place. I did make Alli a bracelet once, though. Mailed it to her with a card that had two beautiful little girls on the front dressed in crisp cotton dresses with mud up to their knees. "We've been through a lot of dirt together," it read. "I drank myself into an arts and crafts class in rehab," I wrote inside. "Beats basket-weaving, I suppose."

I tapped my cigarette on the can and looked over at Jesse. "You were so quiet and shy that first day I met you. You know, when we first got here? So shy."

He scoffed and shook his head. "Because I was messed up. I'd shot up just outside the gate before I came in." He raised his sandaled foot and pointed. "Yep, right there between the toes, just outside the gate up the hill there." He shook his head as if even he couldn't believe it.

"Whoa, Jesse. I don't even know what to say to that."

"It's just fucked up. There's not a word you *could* say to that."

So, I didn't. I remembered how motherly I felt towards him that first day. Lost and confused as a child myself, I still wanted to assure him everything was going to be okay. But I didn't tell him then, nor would I now. I just looked down and played with my cigarette against the edge of the butt can.

"But I didn't get it right the first time I was in here," he said. "I did everything they told us not to do."

"You were here? In this place, before?"

"Yep. And I met a girl, and we got real smart together. We blew these people off and checked out early. Left, *AMA*, as they say. You know, against medical advice. Heroin's her DOC too. But

I've got to get it right this time," he said. "I have to, or my family ... they told me ... this is it. They won't be my family anymore. And see, I'm a mama's boy. You've got a boy, right, Miss Laura?"

"I've got two."

"Well, then you get it. I *love* my mama. And I knew when they told me that – when my family told me that – I knew I had to come back and get it right. If I don't, she won't be my mama anymore. I've worn her out."

"You'll get it if you want it. If you really want it. You know, like they tell us all the time, we've got to be done with it, maxed out, finished. No inkling we can drink or use normally later. They're teaching us what we need to do to get it right in here. We just have to *do* it."

He was staring at his feet, but nodded in agreement.

"You still with that same girl?"

He looked up and smiled. "Yeah, believe it or not, it's actually working."

"She clean?"

"She's at another rehab. They don't let couples go to the same place, you know?"

I actually did know that, now. There were several people who had a partner at another facility.

"But when I told her I had to get clean," he continued, "That I had to have my family in my life, she knew she had to get clean too. So, anyway, we decided to go at the same time, get clean together, whatever."

"That's good. You couldn't do it if one of you was still

138

using."

"Oh, hell no. It's what we do. Well, it's what we did."

"Well, I wish you both the best, and you, the very best. Because even if it doesn't work out with her, family's important. In my family, it's everything."

He dropped his cigarette butt in the can, fired up another, looked off in the distance and continued. "The thing is, I know, and I know better. It's like it's not even me when I'm using. Like it's somebody else, and I'm watching, but I can't stop this thing. Then I'm listening to everyone on my ass. Sucks."

"It does suck."

"I'll tell you what I *did* learn from the first time in here, though," he said, pointing his cigarette at me. "I was in here just long enough the first time to mess things up. Once you know a little about this stuff – getting clean and sober, especially the spiritual stuff – it'll mess up your using." He paused, shook his head and then tapped his smoke against the side of the can. "You can't just go back out, start using again and *un-know* it. Believe me, I tried, but you *can't*. And that spiritual stuff? It just fuckin' sits there on your soul, that's what it does. It'll even fuck up a good high." He shook his head again, put out his cigarette and laughed as he blew the last of his smoke up toward the ceiling fan wobbling at the top of the Butt Hut.

"I guess I can see how that's true," I said. Other people returning from a relapse had told me the same thing.

"But I still used. Oh yeah, because that's how *this* genius rolls!" He poked his thumb in his chest and rolled his eyes. "Makes

139

a lot of sense, right? I kept using, even when it sucked." His smile quickly left as he played with the cigarettes in their pack, then he gazed out at the rolling hillside.

"Makes about as much sense as my drinking does," I said.

"I'm just a junkie," he muttered.

"Yeah, and I'm a drunk, but you're not *just a* junkie, Jesse. You're more than that." I patted him on the shoulder before I even thought about it.

He turned and, for the first time, looked me straight in the eyes. "And you're a mom. And you're a good lady."

I quickly looked away and swallowed back tears. *Was I? Or had anything good I'd ever done been erased by the awful, embarrassing drunk I'd become?* We continued smoking in silence until one of the aides rang the old-fashioned school bell signaling us to put out our smokes and return to the lecture.

*   *   *

There's a lot of good stuff going on when one addicted person talks to another about their truth. Our Community was a microcosm of life, and though our mentors might have only two weeks more sobriety, they were willing to reach back and pull the next person up because they had been there and then pushed through detox and past the bullshit lying and denial that goes along with addiction. It created a safe place to get honest. *Gotta own your shit before you can give it up!* as the younger people were always saying. Maybe I didn't shoot heroin like Jesse, but I did watch, seemingly from the outside, as I drank myself into oblivion, totally baffled every time as to why it always ended the same, messy way. And I did break the hearts of those I loved most. But mostly, I needed my family like he did. So, even though Jesse was a heroin junkie, I now knew we really weren't that different at all.

Chapter 19

No one at home would believe my metamorphosis, even if they were here watching. I marveled at it myself. I woke up *rested* between 4:30 and 5:00 o'clock every morning with no alarm. I would tiptoe to the bathroom, wash my face and brush my teeth, quietly step into my flip-flops, pull my key fob bracelet over my wrist and slip out the door into the morning darkness.

I loved the quiet of the morning. I had no place to be and no assignments yet to complete. I would walk across the parking lot, past the gym and up the sidewalk to the Bodega. Some mornings I would see one of the workers restocking the kitchenette, but most times I was alone, making my coffee in the dimly lit building. There were always a few leftovers strewn about the Bodega, hinting of the night before. A soda can on the rail of the pool table, a fruit bar wrapper on a table, and maybe a couple of AA Big Books left on chairs. Morning-after clean-up was a whole different ballgame in this place!

I could cherish this special morning time because the Head Traffic had ceased. I had finally exited the Highway to Hell. So, in my newly discovered quiet time, I would fix my coffee and step out into one of my favorite moments of the day. I would pause on the front patio of the Bodega and take in God's wakening of the new day. The sun peeked through the trees rising from the creek bed, and the morning air was pure, but full. It smelled of misting sprinkler water, happy flowering plants and their damp dirt underneath, and chlorine from the swimming pool. It smelled like summer. I experienced inner-peace as never before. I felt God's Grace.

I would walk around the side of the building to the Butt Hut. The light was always on in the Hut, and I would position my chairs, prop up my feet, fire up a smoke, and sip my coffee. This was my new routine, starting the day quietly meditating with God.

The skunks and raccoons would argue that the morning had not yet arrived because they were still on night-shift duty, moving about their nosy business in spite of my intrusion. The albino skunk, who looked like someone had turned his coat inside-out, was the most daring. He would look me in the eye and continue his shopping as close as he pleased (or as close as I dared let him) among an occasional candy wrapper or Coke can left behind the night before. We respected each other and went about our individual routines.

Most mornings I would enjoy about fifteen minutes before the men I had grown to love, cherish and respect would start showing up. Kevin always came. He was pretty quiet in the morning, but a good, positive presence for the start of a day. Paul was always there. I loved his sense of humor, and his hunger for a spiritual connection with God was inspiring. He was in a completely different life stage – mid-thirties, father of two small children – but he became one of my best Rehab buddies. Frequent Flier Haney would come at some point, and Ernest was usually there.

Ernest reminded me of the Chief from *One Flew Over the Cuckoo's Nest*. He was a large, dark brown man with pock marks on his face. Like the Chief, he was a soft-spoken man of few words. Ernest was sick the entire time I was in Rehab. Paul would wake to his violent puking at least once a night. Sometimes Ernest would miss meetings because he was genuinely ill, but he made no excuses for it. "It's the drink," he would say. "It may not be *in* me now, but the damage is." I liked him. He had a kind, honest soul.

All in all, I usually started my mornings with four or five men, and we would sit smoking, drinking coffee and quietly discussing our Recovery like a construction crew planning their workday. But our work was a matter of life and death. After our coffee sub-committee meeting, some would head to the top of the hill for morning prayer and meditation. I was getting more than my fair share of group activities, so I would return to the Bodega, refill my coffee and fix a cup for my roommate. She would be stirring when I returned.

Our building was like a motel with ten rooms in a strip at the top of a hill, and our door faced a wide walkway splitting the distance between the Bodega in the main campus area in one direction and a women's dorm at the back of campus in another. It was the same building I had seen rising from the parking lot that first rainy day, and it wasn't sad at all, not even on the backside where our window looked out over the medical area below and the woods and creek beyond where doe brought their fawns to feed in the evening. The inside was dorm-like with hardwood floors, two queen-sized beds, two dressers, two desks, a vanity area and bathroom. It was cleaned every day. We only made our beds, kept the room picked up and did our own laundry down the road at the women's dorm. Pretty good gig. I had prepared myself for scrubbing toilets with a toothbrush.

"You're the best roomy an addict ever had!" Melissa would say through her sleepy smile when I returned with coffee. It felt good to do something kind for someone else first thing in the morning. Then Melissa and I would move about the business of getting ready for the day.

Alli's Pink Bag *had* made it back to me, and one of our never-fail morning routines was checking in on Alli's Pink Bag of Inspiration. The bag had a notebook paper note attached:

"40 Days of Inspiration!"

"You're Amazing!"

"We love you!"

then an arrow drawn, directing me to flip the note, where it read:

"Only One a Day!

"Don't Cheat!"

Every morning Melissa would ask, "What's Alli say today?" and I would grin and dig deep into the Pink Bag of Inspiration like a kid digging for the best candy in a trick-or-treat bag. I would pull out our daily paper square of wisdom, read it aloud and carefully post it on the whiteboard above my dresser with a large, round magnet.

Those phrases from previous days, lovingly written by her on small notebook paper squares, were equally lovingly taped together by me in a long string. That string was also posted on my board, making a long ribbon that draped across my dresser. I liked that as time passed and my paper chain grew longer, I had to gently move it each time I reached into a drawer. I would smile and think of my Alli.

After the words were read, hairdryers and running water would fill the silence and create the silence all at the same time as we pondered the day's phrase and how it applied to our tangled and tortured hearts and souls we were working so desperately to unravel and release so God could put them back together again in the sane, peaceful, spiritual shape He had designed for us all along.

We certainly had nothing to distract us from our thoughts. *No cell phones, computers, iPods, radios or other electronic devices of any kind allowed.* Sometimes the silence was maddening.

Chapter 20

Some mornings I would head down the hill to get my meds while Melissa was getting ready. Meds, shower, blood pressure check, make-up and breakfast happened for me every morning, no matter the order. That was something in and of itself. I was where I needed to be, doing what I needed to do, on time. Miraculous!

Some days my blood pressure was elevated; others, not. The nurses assured me this was normal in early recovery, but I was required to drop by throughout the day for monitoring.

"You know, Miss Verna, my blood pressure is only up when you're on duty. I don't know what that means, it's just an observation."

Another nurse passed by and gave me wink. "It's true, Verna."

"Maybe if you would quit sassing me, it would be normal," Miss Verna would say. "Now sit your sassy butt down. Don't forget I was with you from the beginning, and I don't think you want me to start telling stories ... when you were less sassy ... whining and ..."

"Oh, no ma'am, we don't want that! I *will* miss our times together."

"Hmmph. Just don't miss them enough to bring you back here for another visit, lady."

I took meds every morning and evening, even after I was done detoxing. There was my regular blood pressure medicine, folic acid, vitamins, and a laxative for my never-ending constipation. The medication distribution process provided me with much personal folly. The process itself was funny, and the people-watching was exceptional.

The medication window was just down the sidewalk from SCU. Members of the Community would dutifully line up morning, noon and night to receive their prescribed medications. The line would extend all the way across that same parking lot near the creek where I had entered on a golf cart in the rain my very first day. When we approached the window, we would state our name and security number, and the nurse would pass us a small paper cup containing our meds. We would pour them in our hand, fill the cup at the nearby fountain and then stand before her until we swallowed them all.

"Oh, this is *great!*" I laughed out loud the first time I lined up to receive my meds at the window. I had no idea all this was going on while I was in SCU. No less than forty people were already in line that morning.

"Fantastic! We have our very own *One Flew Over the Cuckoo's Nest* medication window! Where's Nurse Ratched? This is freaking' fantastic!" The older Community members nodded and laughed along with me while the college-aged kids rolled their eyes or shook their heads in confusion.

There were actually two nurses filling the role of our Nurse Ratched. One was a large, cranky androgynous creature and the other, a petite, pleasant young lady who appreciated my sense of humor. Therefore, I very much appreciated her.

"Mornin' Nurse! How goes the drug-dealing business today?"

"Busy as usual, but still not making a dime, Laura."

"Consider the company you're keeping." I would swallow my medications, wish her a good day and move on about my busy schedule.

Turns out, our doctors weren't hacks at all, but leaders in the medical field of addiction, and our medical area was top-notch and quite sophisticated in many ways. If one of the doctors changed our medications, the patient could walk just outside the doctors' offices, across a sidewalk to the med window, ask them to refresh their computer screen, the changes would be noted, and the modified medications would be distributed. I knew this because the doctors were always adjusting my laxative dosage.

*   *   *

"I thought drunks were supposed to have diarrhea when they detox. What's up with that?" I asked the doctor.

"I don't know, but we'll get you straightened out, Laura."

"See, I always knew I'm not like those other people you call alcoholics. I *knew* it! What about that, Doc?"

"Well," he smiled, "I don't know about that."

"Then I'll be unlike those other alcoholics in my bowel, and just another drunk who needs help otherwise. How about that?"

"There ya go. Have a good day, Laura."

*   *   *

One time I mistakenly told the young Nurse Ratched the eldest of our doctors had changed my meds when, in fact, it was his much younger brother, also a doctor there. She took great pleasure letting me know she had ratted me out to the good young doctor.

"Damn, Nurse Ratched!" I said, pounding the counter. "The man prescribes my laxative, for God's sake! You know how far apart the bathrooms are here? He could ruin me with the push of a button on his computer! You know this, right?"

"Oh, yes I do, Laura. Yes I do," she said smiling. Loved her.

I learned a lot about people and addictions just in what I overheard standing in line at the med window. My drug addiction education came mostly from the younger crowd. Some of it was slang, like Benzos, bars, and rails, and other conversations convinced me they could have passed their pharmaceutical boards. They knew which combinations produced the best high and which combinations were dangerous, because no one abusing drugs would want to do something stupid and hurt himself. We were all guilty of that twisted logic. Me, with my Diet Coke and whiskey and low-sodium mixers with my vodka so as not to agitate my high blood pressure. But most times I just enjoyed their youthful ignorance.

"I mean seriously," Taylor said in line one day. "We're all adults here. What's with all the security and the staff wanting to know where I am all the damn time? What is up with that? Where's the trust?" Her peers mumbled sarcastic support.

"Well, last time I checked, this place was teeming with alcoholics and addicts, so ..." I said with a shrug.

"Ha! The lady has a point!" Ken said, pointing to me and laughing.

Ken was the man who had earlier tried to protect my anonymity on the church van. After Rehab, he was taking a road trip to see his children and grandchildren to make his amends in person. He was about five foot seven, a little chubby with dark black hair that he probably dyed. His clothes were very country club golf, and I pegged him as an investor/entrepreneur-type guy.

Some people in Rehab were vague about their careers, and others laid it all out there so wide and flat, I was pretty sure they were creating a more interesting past than they had actually experienced. To be fucked up and quite ordinary otherwise wasn't enough for them. As for me, married twenty-six years, mother of three, legal assistant for twenty-five years, and now a principal's secretary at my old high school, I couldn't have been more ordinary. Well, other than my extraordinary drinking career, and in Rehab, even that was quite ordinary.

I also saw a doctor every morning. We all did. You could go first thing, after breakfast or after the Community Meeting. I ate a big breakfast, headed back down the hill to the medical area and plopped down in the waiting area of the doctors' office. The doctor visits were on a first-come, first-served basis, so the waiting room stayed pretty full, but we had four doctors, so we were in and out pretty quickly.

The college-aged kids were typical, rolling out of bed,

shuffling in wearing their night clothes and flip-flops, then sleeping with their heads back against the wall, mouths open, until someone nudged them for their turn. And although the rest of us were wide awake and dressed for the day, we usually exchanged quiet morning pleasantries. Not this morning, however.

"Well, *today*–not every day–but *today* I'm glad we always see the doctors. Man, I've got some serious diarrhea," Phil said.

"Jealous," I said flatly.

"Having a little difficulty there are we, Laura?" Paul was laughing.

"Hmmph."

"Weeeeelllll, a little irregularity makes the lady cranky!" Paul elbowed the guy sitting next to him, and they snickered like school boys.

"Diarrhea, Phil?" Amy said. "That's got to be rough walking all over this campus all day. That's your body getting straightened out. What was your DOC?"

"Name it," Phil said. "Alcohol mostly, but I had a helluva party going on up in here." He tapped his finger on his temple.

"And now the long-overdue hangover is in your shorts!" Paul said.

"Dude, not cool."

"Again, jealous," I said. "I'd take the place of Masseur Poopie Pants over here for a day at least."

"*Seriously*, people!" Lindy shouted. "Since when do we have conversations, in mixed company, no less, about our bowel movements?"

"Or lack thereof," I mumbled.

"Well," Paul said, pointing around the room. "I know *you* drink til ya puke just so you can drink some more, and *you* like to snort pretty much anything up your nose. She likes needles, and you *all* know I smoke K2 like it's the crack of weed. So, I say, *Seriously, people!* What the hell could be off-limits after all we know about each other, right?"

"*Seriously,*" we answered collectively. Then we went back to staring blankly at the waiting room television and old magazines. Harrison couldn't bear the silence.

"I do not know of these things of which you speak," he said, butchering a British accent with his Texas drawl. He crossed his legs dramatically and popped his magazine for emphasis. "Can you not see," he said, pausing for effect and looking at us over the top of his glasses, "I am trying to read up on the news from last December over here?"

"And sadly," I said, "it probably *is* news to you, ya drunk."

"Back at ya, baby." Harrison chuckled and raised his magazine in front of his face.

"There's so much wrong with all of that," Taylor droned without opening her eyes. She and the other Collegiates were sitting along one wall, heads back, eyes closed.

"It's what you talk about at their age," Josh said, opening one eye to see if anyone would take the bait. "I mean, they're *old.*"

"You listen here, Sonny!" Harrison said, shaking his finger and curling his lips in to look as if he had no teeth. Josh raised the back of his head up off the wall and uncrossed his arms as

Harrison continued. "You are to respect the time I've put in to get me where I am today!" Harrison stretched out his arms in Jesus-like fashion, and nodded his head up and down as he looked proudly around the waiting area.

"Again, so wrong," Taylor added, opening her eyes a bit.

Josh was grinning. "And yet, I arrive at the inevitable finish line in half the time it took you to get here, old man!"

"Aww, screw you."

"Screw *you!*" Josh said standing up and walking towards Harrison. Everyone held their breath and shot nervous glances at each other.

"You going to the men's focused study tonight?" Josh winked at Harrison.

"Yeah."

"See ya there," Josh said, and they both grinned and shook hands as he headed back to the doctors' offices.

"*Rehab,*" Paul said in a deep, dramatic announcer voice. "Where men brag about winning at losing, and where being a quitter is a good thing."

We all smiled and returned to our silent waiting.

*   *   *

Dr. Kirkpatrick was a soft-spoken guy with a quiet confidence who smiled a lot. We liked all the doctors, but everyone in the Community agreed Kirkpatrick was a sweet, quiet soul.

"So, you're doing good, Laura ... I mean, are you doing good?" He rolled his chair towards me and sat bending forward with his arms on his legs, hands clasped, looking me straight in the eyes. He never sat behind his desk.

"Yes sir, I'm doing good."

He picked up a brochure from his desk. "You know that we can help you quit smoking, right? Has anyone told you that?"

I nodded yes.

"It's a good environment to quit. If there are any complications with the cessation medications or any of your other medications, you see a doctor daily, so we can recognize it and make adjustments quickly. Hopefully, you've become spiritually connected through your Twelve Step work. That helps. And you're in a busy routine, which we've found also helps create a successful environment.

"So, do you think this might be something you're interested in, Laura? Quitting smoking?"

"No. I'm not ready."

"Well, I understand that. And, as you obviously know, if you're not ready, you won't be successful. So, if you change your mind, just let me or one of the other doctors know, okay? We, of course, would like to see you quit."

"Well, quite frankly, Doc, now you're just being greedy," I said. "So, let's review, shall we?"

"Oh, let's do." He grinned and sat up straight on the edge of his chair.

"One," I began counting on my fingers. "Giving up the booze, right?" He smiled and nodded in agreement. "Right ... okay. Two, I'm surrendering my will to God. Now, that surrender thing, that's a biggie, Doc ... for me, anyway."

"Understandable." He leaned back in his chair and crossed his arms, as if to get comfortable for the remainder of the show.

"Next, I'm working my Twelve Steps in AA. Now, that's no check, check, check-off easy thing," I said, making check marks in the air. "You don't just whip right through that, so ... "

"Agreed."

"Okay. And ... Oh! And let's not forget! All this," I said, waving my arms dramatically. "*All* of this, while I'm sifting through a massive pile of shit in therapy!" He's laughing out loud now. "I'm working on some pretty heavy stuff here, Doc, and yet, you still want more!" I raised my fists in mock desperation, and shouted, "You can't have my smokes! It's ... it's all I've got left, man!" He set the brochure back on his desk, applauded softly and wished me a good day. I gave him a wink in return and left his office.

Everyone was staring as I entered the lobby. "Tell Dr. Kirkpatrick 'No!' Just trust me on this. No matter what he says, or what he asks from you, just go Nancy Reagan on his ass, and 'Just say No.' He's a mean, brutal man. *Brutal*, I say!" I dramatically tossed my head and rushed out the door, leaving bewilderment in my wake.

I would have never scratched and clawed my way through the tough stuff to face the truth about myself without these people. In our isolation in the hills, we had nothing behind us. No past, no ulterior motives. And there was nothing between us but our desperate need to heal. Being plucked from family and a small town of lifelong friends freed me to seek my truth without fear of judgment or shame. It was a chance to find the Me that God had always intended before the people, places and work of life shaped me. Before the drink drowned me.

My community taught me to give up myself and to give of myself, and in doing so a trusting exchange was put into motion. All our dark things could be shared without judgment, and no matter how sick, sad, mean or selfish, they neither increased nor decreased one's value as a human being in our Community. It was a safe place for me to do the work for my sobriety.

I received immeasurable wisdom and support in conversations that were seemingly happenstance, disguised as smoke breaks or random seating at meals. But they weren't random at all – they were my life lessons – my gifts, given to me by God, through what I would have once thought the most improbable of people and circumstances. They were gifts to me, from Him, through his people, because no matter how busted up and broken, we were all still His.

I can't recover if I don't move closer to God, they said, and I can't get closer to God with shame in the way. Shedding the dark things is necessary to move closer to God and to recovery, and I had to walk through the dark to get to the light.

We can neither love or be loved if our secrets are in the way. It's the side of me that I refuse to look at that rules me. I must be willing to look at the dark side in order to heal my mind and heart. Because that is the road to freedom. I must walk into darkness to find the light and walk into fear to find peace. By revealing my secrets and ridding myself of guilt I can actually change my thinking. By altering my thinking, I can change myself. My thoughts create my future. What I will be tomorrow is determined by what I think today.

The process of finding my truth wasn't one of shiny self-affirmations in front of an ornate mirror. It was more like digging out an old mirror that had been banged around in my purse every drunken day of my life and trying to see myself through all the scratches and smears in its fading reflection. It was difficult, but I knew I was in there somewhere because I had survived. Many don't, they told us.

And ready or not, I found the truth about me—so selfish, always better-than. Working so hard to look better than you, I couldn't see your needs. So self-seeking that whoever and whatever were around me was never enough. The drunk. It was a heart-wrenching realization but essential to my healing, for these were the very traits that kept me discontent, wandering around in my What Now? Life without purpose, seeking temporary solace in alcohol.

The beauty of it, for me, was that once I finally knew what

158

the hell was wrong with me, I didn't even have to fix it myself.
God would do that with one, simple condition. I had to let Him.

Chapter 21

My treatment consisted of education about the disease of alcoholism, how addiction affects and operates in the brain, AA 12-Step Studies and meetings, then therapy. Therapy was a separate deal. That was made very clear. You could sort out your mommy and daddy issues, unhealthy or abusive relationships, work and financial problems, but it was made very clear, none of these caused substance abuse.

"Did you drink when you were happy?" Joe would ask. "How about when you were sad? Had money? Broke? You drink no matter what! There's nothing outside you causing you to drink. You drink no matter what the hell else is going on outside you. And you know what's going on outside you? Life. It's just life, people! And other people go through lives just like yours without drinking and using."

That's got to be some kind of sorcery I'm not privy to.

Who decided which people were put into group therapy together was a mystery until the day before I left and they pulled back the curtain a bit. My group was all ladies -- the only one like it on campus. Some were weeks ahead of me in Rehab, others came in with me, and one or two came in just before I left. We were single, married, young, old, addicts, alcoholics, poor and rich. But in our group, we were one.

As we gathered in our small group therapy, we grabbed a clipboard loaded with the same form each day asking us to describe our mood, how we perceived our progress in Recovery, and our goals for the day and the week. Sometimes Julianne gave us a prompt and the discussion began. Today's opening topic was, "What has surprised you most about yourself or the treatment process since you've been here?" Amy went first.

"It's so true about my using being more than when I'm actually doing it, or when I'm high, you know? I mean, when Joe was talking about the mental obsession, that was it for me. I think about syringes, I think about hooking up to get some, about fixing it. I mean, I use in my dreams, so when he said that stuff, I wanted to use so bad!" She was crying.

"I mean, I wanted to be *doing that!* I'm glad I'm here and all. I want to stay clean, I really do. I've tried before, but I really want to get it right this time."

The desperation in her voice had me feeling anxious. I feared she might flip out, storm out, give up, or something. But she stayed in her seat and continued on.

"But when I start thinking about that stuff he said, about it being more than just getting high, it was like I was *there*. I wanted to *be there*, fixing up my junk, getting ready to get high. It was more about the getting ready than thinking about how it felt to be high, you know?"

"I do know," I said. "I was blown away. I know this sounds crazy, but I could *smell it*. I mean actually *smell* whiskey! That's crazy! I started thinking about getting bottles out of the cabinet, the mixers, the glasses, everything. But *smelling whiskey?* I wasn't ready for that. That just came out of nowhere! Blindsided me, really."

"I can totally relate to that." It was Ryan, tossing her bleached hair back out of her eyes and pursing her pouty lips. Ryan was an exotic beauty in her early twenties. Marilyn Monroe with a slutty edge. She was petite, but whether by pedigree or purchase, all the parts had made it into the package, and she dripped with sexuality. I had pondered whether she was just plain sexy or if she had learned somewhere along the way to use her sexuality to get what she wanted, and now it was simply all she thought she was. But I dismissed it. *I'm not her mother or her shrink. I've got my own problems to work out.*

The collegiate boys followed her around like a dog in heat. Paul said she enjoyed leading the young guys on. "I mean, I get it," he said. "I totally get it, sad as it is to watch. I'm just old enough to know what she's doing isn't even fair to those young guys." Rumor had it she was a porn star. The married men always phrased it this way. "The young guys say she's a porn star. I mean . . . *I* don't know, but . . ."

Ryan continued. "I mean, I like the whole process of the hook up, and I liked counting my bars to see how many I had and figuring up how long I think it will last. Of course, I have friends who will give me anything I want." She broke a coy smile. "And I mean *anything*! That's a big part of my problem."

162

She licked her puffy pink lips and continued. "But, you know, I would deliver for them too, that's how I earned my stuff sometimes, and I liked being the hook up for other people too. Sometimes I would just spread them all over my table and run my fingers over them. *Yeah.*" She looked far off as if she were replaying it in her mind. In my mind, Marilyn Monroe was leaning her buxom chest over a glass table, running her fingers through diamonds.

But I could relate to what Ryan was saying too. I would get edgy about eight-thirty at night and double-check the liquor cabinet. If needed, a quick run to the liquor store would happen to beat the nine o'clock closing because I could not be stranded without it. Alcoholic or addict, we all need our stash.

Ryan continued. "So I get the thing that Joe was saying about it being more than just getting high. It's the whole thing," she said, making a large circle in the air with her long index fingernails. Then she placed one hand across her bosom so she could feel it heave as she let out a heavy sigh.

Good thing our group was all ladies. She used "hook up" way too many times for any mixed company, far from home, longing for a conjugal visit.

Chapter 22

My small group therapy was as if I had hand-picked the people in it. Well, but for one. Theresa was one of The Housewives. She was an irritant.

The Housewives were three women who came in around the same time I did, give or take a day or two. I called them The Housewives in my head because they seemed to have so little going on in their lives that their tiny problems were blown out of proportion and their glaring ones, blown off completely.

"These meds just aren't doing much for me, you know? I mean, I'm not irritable, and I'm sleeping fine, but they just aren't really working for me. I'm going to see the doctor this afternoon. I mean, like, I'm paying a lot for this place, and they should do what I want, you know?"

Or, "Keith really likes my hair darker. Oh, no! Keith would not be my husband. It's a young man who lives three doors down from me. Do you know that group Three Doors Down? Keith and I like that group. Isn't that funny? Keith and I laugh about that. Yes, Keith likes my hair darker. Maybe I can have something done with this dreadful hair when we go into town for the nail salon," stroking her hair and looking off like some stupid dreamy-eyed teenage girl.

Come to find out, that Housewife was having sex with Mr.

Three Doors Down, and the leaders in her church thought it necessary she include details in her confession of their extramarital activities.

"I mean, I understand because I was born and raised in that church, and they ask it in a loving way, and all. It's just so embarrassing, them asking 'Did you perform oral sex?' and things like that."

Rachel's sudden and stealth appearance in such conversations was uncanny. "And do these church leaders, these holy men, these frustrated farts—do they drape a table cloth down the front of the desk of judgment before asking you to repeat the details of your sexual sin? Or do they have one of those desks with a privacy panel built in so they don't even have to bother wearing pants to the show?" Rachel, Hypocrisy Police Chief.

But her sexual indiscretions were never mentioned in our group therapy. It was never even acknowledged. She shared her one, true heart-wrenching conflict one day at the Butt Hut. "My boys are coming for Family Weekend. I won't be able to smoke at all. I mean, what is this?" She held her cigarette in front of her as if a stranger had just stuffed it between her fingers in a tobacco drive-by. "I mean, I really don't smoke cigarettes at all!"

Yeah, see, you really do. All day, every day. What you don't do, is buy cigarettes. That's why I have to avoid your ass. I don't want your dollar bill. I can't smoke a dollar bill. So, take the plunge, try some honesty and admit you're a smoker. You can do it! People are accepting and admitting to things around here all the time! Then put some money in an envelope and write the name of a brand you've been bumming on the outside of it. They bring cigarettes back from town almost daily. Irritant.

She tapped her cigarette with her index finger. She always looked awkward, like a school kid trying to look cool. "My boys would just die. They're both very athletic, and they see me working out all the time. Omagosh! They would just die if they saw me smoking. Truly, they would die."

Not that you would return home at two o'clock in the morning covered in scratches with leaves in your hair after drunk-hiking through the woods in the middle of the night. Yeah, smoking. That would be the deal-breaker.

Another Housewife had some kind of Knots Landing bullshit going on at home. All the ladies in her neighborhood were obsessed with who was wearing what designer and who was driving what type of vehicle. She, of course, was not; she just chose to talk about it incessantly. That Housewife liked Xanax and booze, and her husband liked pot and booze. They had a nasty domestic incident that landed her in jail, judicially separated from her children and now in Rehab. One could argue she was in Rehab solely to mitigate her damages.

The third Housewife was a masterpiece of plastic surgery puffery from her lips, to her boobs, to her bottom. No further description can be provided because, frankly, that's all there was to her. She was simply a curvaceous void.

The Housewives moved through their days as a single unit, and they were flawlessly interchangeable to the blind eye as they discussed the heady topics of clothes removed from their bags by the staff at check-in, having been deemed too provocative, lack of performance in their current medications and non-recovery topics such as hair and busy days at the gym and spa after dropping off their children. Hence, in my head, they were The Housewives.

Chapter 23

Each week, one of our four physicians gave a lecture on addiction. They were my favorite of the lectures. Dr. B. Daniels was lecturing on addictions and pathways in the brain, but first, he had some behavioral issues to discuss, he said.

"This is off today's scheduled topic," he said, trying to make eye contact with as many as possible throughout the room. "But it's important, and it's an issue I need to address."

Some looked at each other and shrugged, others of us knew exactly where the Good Doctor was going, and all of us sat up a little bit straighter.

"There is talk all over campus ... well, there is concern all over campus as well ... Just let me say this. If you want to go up on the hill, hide out on the trails, or wherever and make out or hide out somewhere else on campus and hook up, that's your business. We're all adults here, and you can do whatever you decide to do. Work a thirteenth step, whatever you want to call it.

"But if you want to get well, if you are serious about your recovery, don't do this thing. You are not in a healthy position to be taking on a relationship."

The young suspects just stared straight ahead.

"There are people in here I recognize who are back from relapse. A few of them will tell you starting a relationship in rehab is a bad idea. They'll tell you even having sex just for the sake of having sex, while you're in here, is a bad idea. Truth is, you're probably chasing a feeling, a euphoria, if you will, that your brain is missing because you're clean.

"It won't end well, and it will probably get pretty ugly even before it ends. Furthermore, and most importantly, it's a distraction from your recovery. I mean, let's all be honest here. You know where you are emotionally and physically. You know your life isn't in the best of order. Well, you're a mess!"

Lots of confirming laughter from The Community.

"Why would you think anyone else in here is any different than you? Is this really a good place to go searching for a healthy relationship?"

More laughter from The Community, mostly the older members.

"For the life of me, I've never understood why two people think, 'Well, if I take my smelly pile of stuff and combine it with your smelly pile, it's going turn into something that smells pretty.' It's just not going to happen, people!

"So again, you can do whatever you want to do, but I must caution you – if you want to get well, don't do this thing. Just don't do it."

Some of the young people looked at each other and rolled their eyes. I suspected most of the adults were secretly wishing they *were* getting a hook-up. It would probably be an excellent tension-breaker. But there weren't any indiscretions in the adult community, at least not to my knowledge. I found it surprising, considering you had alcoholics and addicts who had no doubt damaged their relationships at home, who were now surrounded by people who understood their pain and isolation and who could vanish from their lives in thirty days.

The doctor returned to his scheduled lecture on addictions and the brain. It was fascinating and also very helpful in my Recovery. Understanding the progression of my alcoholism helped me accept my plight and how to interpret and correct my jacked-up thinking. His clinical explanation of why I had lost the choice of whether or not to drink before I came in, allowed me to forgive myself somewhat. It wasn't a matter of weakness or poor character. I took one particular part of this lecture and internally translated it into lay terms I could understand.

I thought of my drinking as exercise for certain pathways in my brain. I had given my addiction muscles one hell of a workout over the years and a lot of memory for those muscles to draw upon. Their game whistle was booze, but they were good-to-go even before the actual game began. That's where the mental obsession I'd learned about came into play. My plotting and planning were my stretching and warming up. My pregame activities.

I had to learn to retrain those muscles by learning new habits and reinforcing them through routine. I had to let them sleep by not feeding them because even one drop of alcohol would stimulate them, and the madness of my addiction would be off and running. My drinking muscles would then let it be known that one drink is absolutely unacceptable, and they'll be quivering and edgy until they get more.

But if I bypass those addiction muscles and use others over and over again (coping mechanisms non-addicts use all the time) the addiction muscles will become less dominant. However, they will always lay dormant, waiting for stimulus. I could wrap my head around that, which made total abstinence acceptable to me.

In winding up his lecture, Dr. Daniels said, "So those of you who are thinking once you're all straightened out from treatment and you've got your DOC under control that you can go home and smoke some marijuana? Sorry. Yes, even marijuana will stimulate that part of your addicted brain, and the cycle of abuse will eventually start all over again."

Oh, the moans and groans that filled that room! I had to laugh. Pot was never my thing, but obviously there *were* a lot of people who were looking forward to smoking a big fat joint once they got out of Rehab. Sorry, Charlie. No can-do.

Heather groaned the loudest, and then yelled, "You're killin' me, Doc! You're really killing me! Right here, right now." Dr. Daniels smiled, and everyone was laughing, some making pot-smoking gestures with their finger to their lips.

"Damn it, Doc!" Josh said, pointing at Heather. "I had a hook up in Hawaii! Heather is from Hawaii, you know."

Heather was as exotic as her island home. She had thick, curly hair that spiraled down to her butt—a short trip, as she was only about five feet tall, but impressive all the same. She was a natural beauty with almond brown skin, crystal blue eyes and large, full lips. She was a nurse with an appetite for narcotics, and the buffet was always open at her job in the hospital.

One day in our small group therapy, Julianne started with "Anyone here have anything in particular they want to talk about or get off their chest?" and Heather unloaded.

"Well, I think it's absolute bullshit what they've done to me here." She sat still, waiting for reinforcement. It appeared Julianne knew what she was talking about, and possibly some of the people in our group, but I was clueless. I adjusted myself in my chair and waited for someone else to take the bait.

"What's going on, Heather?"

"Well," she said, clearing her throat and sitting up straight in her chair, preparing for her presentation. "You know how they do the family thing? You know what I'm talking about? Your family comes, and they learn all about addicts and all about you and your addiction. All that family therapy crap? You know what I'm talking about. Well, I didn't want that, and I made that *very* clear when I came in this place. No family time.

"I mean, you people can do what you want. Do what you think you need to do, but that's not for me. By the time I found out administrators sent an invitation *against my will*, my family had already made flight reservations! They had a hotel room in town, for God's sake!"

She was screaming and crying now. Everyone was silent. Some leaned forward to show their interest and sympathy. I picked up one of the squishy stress balls from the coffee table and kept my spectator seat.

"I'm a goddamn nurse, and I know they can't do that! This

is a violation of my privacy! I'm a grown woman, and I didn't want them here. It's *my* fucking rehab, and I don't want them here! Does anyone even care about that?"

The group nodded and whispered confirmations that they did indeed care. Heather was frantically wiping her face, over and over with trembling hands. She wiped snot on her floral sundress, tossed back her long, curly hair and shook her head in disbelief. No one offered a tissue. The rules.

"I can't trust these people with my treatment!" she wailed. "I can't trust, so I can't be treated by these people!" She grabbed a tissue box and continued. "So ... I'm leaving. I'll have to find some way to reimburse my parents for their travel expenses, but I have to leave. I cannot trust my treatment to these people any longer."

Heather smoked in her room. She sneaked in a phone somehow. I heard her playing music on it when I had to go to her door one day. She begged me not to tell. Again, not my Program, not my problem. Personally, I'd decided for once in my life, the rules do apply to me. *All* the rules. I had made a conscious decision to do what I was asked to do and be where I was asked to be. On time, even.

Julianne asked me in my individual therapy if Heather's yelling and cursing had upset me. "No. I felt badly she was so upset, but no, it didn't upset me personally."

"Is there anything about what she said or how the group reacted that you need to talk about?"

"Well, it's really not my place to judge what she's doing one way or the other. I mean, I realize that. But do I have an opinion about it anyway? Sure I do."

"Do you want to tell me what that is?"

"Personally, I think it's an excuse," I said with a shrug.

"An excuse?"

"I think it's an excuse not to finish. It's the blame game. Everyone in here's guilty of it. I mean, I did it all the time. I told myself, 'If my job settles down,' or 'When I get used to the kids being gone, then I won't drink so much.' Stuff like that.

"So, if this place has done her wrong in some way, she has an excuse to leave – to not finish the work. Then, in her mind, it's not her fault, and she didn't quit. Meanwhile, she's kept her family out of the loop, so they can't talk to her about what she did or didn't do while she was here."

Julianne smiled slightly, crossed her legs and leaned forward, signaling me to continue.

"I'm not trying to be a bitch, and she can do whatever she wants to do because it doesn't affect my sobriety one way or the other. But yeah, I think it's possible she's crawfishing. If that's the case, then that's what I've learned from it."

"What, specifically, have you learned from it?" she asked.

"Me, personally? I'm done with excuses. It's embarrassing, all the excuses I made! All my justification ... all that shit. When I think about it now, it's all just so sick and embarrassing."

Julianne made a few notes and then looked up. "Are you committed to finishing your stay here?"

"Absolutely."

"Well, that's the most important thing. So, if you are

satisfied with our discussion, we can move on."

"I'm good with it."

Chapter 24

The phones in our rooms were only open from noon to one in the afternoon, then seven to ten-thirty in the evenings. Incoming callers could only leave a message for us to call them back. The facility reserved the right to record or screen calls and messages.

Melissa wasn't sure if they had monitored her calls or if her dad had told them who she should and shouldn't speak with. Nevertheless, some of her calls stopped after a while. When she first arrived, she would tie up the phone most of the evening. After she talked with her dad, stepmom and kids, she would have other conversations that took place with her back to me, her head down and her voice very low. Sometimes they would get heated, and she would shout things like, "You were there too, so don't give me any shit about it anymore!" or "*No*. I don't know how you can hook up with them. Do you not understand where the hell I am? It's *over!*"

I usually left the room when her back faced me and the low-talking began because I just couldn't and wouldn't deal with the stress of even the one-half of those conversations I could hear. I never said a word to her or anyone else about them. I would just grab my smokes and my study materials and head out. I liked to smoke while studying, but reading in the Butt Hut was impossible for me. Though my concentration improved after detoxing, I still couldn't focus enough to tune out all the conversations. The Collegiates always got loud and often down-right offensive. That's saying something after all I'd heard since arriving. Most of them were addicts, rather than alcoholics, and one of the truths I learned in Rehab was alcoholics lie about how much they drank, and addicts exaggerate about how much they used. That was certainly my experience at the Butt Hut, so when the young addicts began their bragging and one-upsmanship, I would escape to my quiet reading place.

There was rarely anyone on the bench outside the SCU where I smoked when I first arrived, and those who did come to smoke were detoxing in SCU, and they were quiet, possibly because they were medicated, but more likely, they were stupefied at their entire situation. Either way, they weren't on my bench long, and I found I could smoke and read there with very little disturbance.

It was there that I met Mark P. late one afternoon. I was sitting cross-legged on my bench, smoking and reading when I looked up and saw him walking towards me from the medical building. He was a tall, slender guy in his late forties, wearing a crisp, white button-down and jeans. He had a cigarette hanging from his mouth, and as he reached in his starched jeans for his lighter, he saw me and pulled the smoke from his mouth.

"Well, hello! Is this where I can smoke?" he asked. *Wow! What a smile.*

"Well, hello to you, and yes it is!" I cleared my throat and tried to regroup. "I'm Laura."

"Mark." He flashed that smile again.

I closed my book, uncrossed my legs down and extended my hand. When he reached down to shake my hand, I saw that his short, gray hair brought out the blue in his eyes, and his skin was a weathered brown with the perfect number of creases. *He's just worn enough to show he knows what the hell.* His hands shook as he lit his cigarette. Boy, could I relate to that!

"So you just get here?" I asked, trying to keep the stupid grin off my face.

"Yeah, a couple of hours ago. I finally just had to take a smoke break. It's a lot, you know what I mean?"

"Oh, I do. It's a helluva lot." I began gathering my study materials that were strewn all over the bench, and stacked them neatly beside me. *I am smiling like a stupid school girl. What the hell?*

"How long have you been here, if you don't mind me asking. I don't really know how this stuff goes ... you know, what you can ask, what not to." He laughed and said, "Never done *this* before, that's for sure."

"Right. Well, I've been here ..." I had to pause and count it up because I had lost track of time, which was weird, because I had been meticulously counting the days since I arrived. "Let's see. Yeah, I've been here about three weeks, and yes, it's perfectly okay for you to ask. You'll be surprised at all the things that are just asked and said – right out there to talk about – once you've been here a bit."

178

"I can imagine. It's a little much already with all they're asking about in there," he said glancing over his shoulder at the SCU.

"Are you going to stay in SCU for a while?"

"Yeah. They tell me they want to watch me at least one night."

"It's not so bad, really. So, I drink. You?"

"Same. And boy, do I drink!" he said laughing nervously, then dragging on his smoke. "Wasn't always like that, but that's where I find myself now." He blew smoke through a heavy sigh and continued. "Yeah, the wife's had enough." He turned and stared out at the trees and the dry creek bed as he smoked. I checked his Wrangler butt before he turned back around and said, "Truth is, I know *she's* had enough, but I've had enough myself." I nodded in agreement, and we let the silence lay there for a bit, and it wasn't the least bit awkward.

"It's hard to tap-out," I said.

He chuckled a bit. "That's a good way to put it. It *is* hard to tap-out." He was sitting next to me now, leaning forward on his knees, looking down at his boots. He flicked his cigarette butt out into the parking lot and rubbed his hands together. Then he clasped them to hold them still.

"Well, you're in a very good place – at least it has been for me," I said. "They're very good here. They know what they're doing, and they're very good to you. I'm already so much better."

"Thanks for that. That's good to hear."

I lit up a smoke, then he lit up another, and we both stared straight ahead smoking together in silence. After a few minutes, he stood, put his smokes in his shirt pocket and wiped his hands on his jeans. He leaned over and placed his tanned, leathery hand on top of mine for a few seconds, gave it a quick, friendly pat and turned to leave. *They're just perfect. You know he's worked hard, but he keeps 'em clean.*

"Well, good to meet you, Laura ... considering, you know," he said flashing that smile again. "Thanks for everything. Really. You've been more helpful than you know."

"You'll be glad you came here," I said. "You'll be good."

"Thanks for that. I'm glad I met you first."

Yeah, well, me too. I think.

"Good luck to you. Good to meet you too," I said.

Well, hell. That's got to be the end of that! Damn.

Two days later I saw Mark as I was walking from the medical area to breakfast. He was standing in the intersection of two walkways at the bottom of the hill with his hands in his jean pockets, turning left, and then right.

"Good morning!" I said as I walked up from behind. "You're lost, aren't you?" I smiled and patted him on the back, but when he turned, I saw his suntanned face had faded to an ashen gray, and his blue eyes looked faded, confused and tired. "It's okay," I said, grabbing his arm. "I wandered around like this for *days*, and you couldn't be near the drunk I was when I got here." His tired face was blank, so I smiled again, and gave his arm a tug. "Let's get up the hill to breakfast, and I'll introduce you to some of the guys." No flash of that beautiful smile. We moved slowly with

Mark plodding his heavy feet up the hill as others breezed by, some heading up for breakfast, others down for meds and a doctor's visit. "It's no wonder you feel lost," I said. "All these limestone buildings with their red rooftops, they all look alike."

I gave him some pointers as we passed through the cafeteria line, and then we headed over to a large group of men. "Excuse me, guys, this is Mark. He's new, and I told him y'all would help him out." They quickly made space at their table and stood to shake his hand. "They will take great care of you," I said, but he didn't hear me. They were already in the middle of the usual introductions. Alcohol. Pasadena. Pretty good so far, thanks.

It was still early, which meant there were mostly only men in the cafeteria. I sat alone near a window and watched deer feed as I ate my breakfast. I had been in long enough to know the social nuances in my little Community. The married men and women never ate together. Too intimate, I suppose. And the young people never mixed with the old when in large groups. Not cool, I knew.

Chapter 25

Eventually, there were conversations about how each one of us came to be in Rehab, and some were dramatic with wailing and gnashing of teeth and others arrived with a whimper. We got there. The only issue was whether or not we, as individuals, were willing to get on with it. Spencer, for example, who became one of my favorite people, was in his seventies, I guessed. He was tall, thin and bald. When we were both early Newcomers, he looked like Ichabod Crain. His entire wrinkly face was drawn in towards his large nose, and he spoke to no one. Cranky old bastard. But as he detoxed, he transformed into the kind, funny grandfather figure I came to know and love. I walked up on a conversation between him and some other men one afternoon.

"If that isn't that damnedest thing," he said chuckling and shaking his head.

"What's up, Spence?"

"I was just telling the guys here that my family did one of those intervention things to get me here. And see, my wife's never worked a day in her life, so turns out, I paid for it! Damnedest thing I ever heard of!"

"That's pretty messed up, Spence. Damn!" Harrison said.

"Well, I do want to see my grandkids, and that wasn't happening anymore. I'll tell you another mess of it all. I'd just made a big trip to the liquor store. You know the one, where you stock up?"

We all smiled and nodded. Hell yeah, we knew the one! Few things felt finer than the big trip to the liquor store, and nothing felt more secure than being stocked up.

"Got the finest Scotch, my favorite, half gallon," he continued. "Then I got any kind of liquor that anybody –whoever came over – would ever want. Just completely stocked the bar. Sure did."

The men kept smiling and nodding their heads, as if they were discussing a pecan pie after the very last piece had been taken. Or maybe their fondness was more that of a good lay from their past, before they were all married. Nice to remember, but those days were over.

"Hope my wife didn't throw all that out. That would surely be a shame." He shook his head again and laughed at the irony of it all. "She should give it to our neighbors. They like to come over in the summer and have a drink on the patio." He stared off, smiling at the thought. "Yeah, it shouldn't go to waste. She should give it to our neighbors." His voice trailed off as he looked down and played around in the dirt with his foot.

"And they talked about their leftover booze as if it were a coat for a neighbor's needy child," I said. "Whatayagonna do, Mr. Spence? Whatayagonna do?" I smiled, patted him on the back and headed into the Butt Hut.

His wife came for Family Week a couple of weeks later. She was a beautiful woman with a precious, spunky personality. "I must say, Mr. Spence," I said, winking at his wife, "Your wife is beautiful! This may be the most serious case of over-marriage I have ever seen!"

"It is that, Laura. You are sure right about that," he said smiling. He sat down next to her, and they held hands. *Adorable. He's going to be a wonderful granddaddy.*

Chapter 26

It was another mandatory evening AA Meeting, and I was not feeling the fellowship. I don't know if was the heat or because I had work to do back in my room – work that had to be done before I would even be considered for release. Whatever the case, everyone else must have been feeling the same because the Bodega was unusually quiet as the leaders headed up front to start the meeting. Then a screech from the back of the room.

"Can someone help me, please?" Every head snapped in her direction, not just for her words, but her voice. We didn't know that voice.

"If you know how ... do *something, please!*" Her pleas broke into sobs, and we exchanged desperate glances as we searched the room for a Newcomer to match with the voice.

"I'm sorry," she said clearing her throat. "I'm Raelynn, alcoholicaddict." And then we found her in the back, near the door, and my heart sank. You had to be eighteen to get in our Rehab, and I suspected she either lied or drove down on her birthday.

I didn't realize what a clean looking crew we were until I saw her. Her strawberry blonde hair was a sticky mess, and her clothes were thrift store faded and rumpled. Her face was worn, way too worn to match her young voice and body.

"He called me his dirty rag!" she cried. *Oh, God no.* I flinched and looked down at my feet, physically ill. "He *always* called me that!" she wailed. I glanced up and saw some staring down at their shuffling feet and others looking helplessly desperate to help. *What the hell do you say to that?*

"Please don't pity me ..." she went on. "I need to get clean and sober, and I've got this crap. I just need someone to help, if you can ... because he ..."

"Because he's a sonofabitch," Rachel said matter-of-factly, and then she slammed her chair against the wall as she stood. Startled, our focus shifted to Rachel. She ran her hands through her spiked hair, placed them on her boney hips and let out a heavy sigh. "Yeah," she said to no one in particular, "I know exactly what the fuck is going on here." She bit her bottom lip and nodded her head for a moment like she was posturing for a fight, then everyone in the room seemed to fade away as we stared in silence as Rachel stomped her thick, black boots up one side of the room, across the front and all the way down the other side to the back where she stood by Raelynn. She hitched up her jeans, let out a heavy sigh and slid into the chair next to her.

"Shhh," she whispered as she wrapped her arms around Raelynn and began gently rocking and stroking her hair. And in the midst of the sobbing and rocking, gothic glory tangled up with faded cotton, I saw her – past her painted body and fuck-you attitude – I saw Rachel. A part of, no longer apart from. A partner in a united front.

I don't know if Rachel's face and demeanor truly softened,

or if maybe I softened. I know those two were inseparable after that. First a quiet pair of survivors, then a couple of giggling girls whispering and sharing candy during meetings. God, I felt blessed to witness that moment – that connection we all seek. To find another trudging through life, dragging along their own bag of dark stuff. Someone we can trust with our secrets. To feel safe. To be understood.

Chapter 27

I was the first of our small discharge group to arrive for our last meeting with Joe in the Bodega. Without the Community, the room seemed church-like with its high ceilings and the mid-morning sun streaming across the floor. There were no buzzing conversations or random outbursts of laughter. No Newcomers spilling coffee, and no Viv in the back smiling and urging us to our seats. Part of me wanted to turn on the lights and shake the place back to life, but instead, I sat near the front and closed my eyes. Time that once seemed insurmountable was suddenly gone, and this most profound of experiences would be indescribable to anyone on the outside. My roomie's sleepy smile when I brought her coffee. Sweet Jesse and his now sparkling eyes. Nurse Ratched laughing and looking over her bifocals as she passed my pill cup. Rachel without her cloak. Joe's knowing grin.

I was going to miss Joe. The way he took giant strides back and forth across the front of the Bodega, yelling and banging the whiteboard like a football coach. The way he hitched up his pants before he made a really strong point. I was going to miss the way he described my drunken despair, my hopelessness – even my busy, crazy head – so vividly, I knew *he* knew. Passionate, repetitive ol' Joe. He would be whipping some other foggy Newcomers into admission while I was winding my way home through the Hill Country.

The familiar buzz began filling the room as the rest of my group filtered in and we exchanged email addresses, phone numbers, and war stories. We wriggled into our seats at the front like excited school children, ready on time, waiting for Joe. Behind us, eighty or more empty chairs. Everyone couldn't go home yet.

Joe hit the threshold. "Good morning!" he shouted, bounding through the doorway and heading up front. "How are you treating the world today, huh?" He had a mischievous smile, and I sometimes lamented we'd never drunk together. He began his signature pacing, looking us over good, as if inspecting his troops. Everyone grinned and sat up straight.

"Well, well, well ... just look at you!" he said shaking his head. "Who would have believed *this* when you crawled in here?" He pointed up and down our row. "Everybody's so clean and shiny ... all sober and shit."

We could hardly believe it ourselves, and as we smiled through bittersweet tears, our lingering glances shared the unspoken. No matter how long we'd been in, or how anxious we were to head home, leaving the bubble of Rehab was scary stuff.

Joe shoved his hands in the pockets of his khaki shorts and lowered his head. He paced the full width of the building and back, then stopped. Everything stopped when Joe stopped – the laughing, the shuffling, maybe even our breathing.

"If you didn't listen to anything I've said before, please hear me now," he said. "Your lives depend on it." I placed my things under my chair and locked eyes on him.

189

"Remember the facts about your disease. It's tough out there," he said, pointing out to the hillsides. "You've got to be prepared. Being strong within yourself didn't work before, and it won't work when you leave here." He turned and stood behind the podium. "You've Got. To. Be. Spiritually. Fit." he said, banging his palm on the podium with each word.

"I want you to look at the person to your left. Now, to your right. Only one of you is going to make it with continuous sobriety when you leave here."

Silence.

"Who are *you* going to be?" he asked. "I don't mean to be discouraging. It's just reality, statistics. Now, if you guys want to go out there and defy some statistics – go out there and prove a bunch of people wrong, then *get after it!* That defiant attitude comes naturally to you people anyway."

No one laughed or even smiled. I looked left, then right, then down at my hands. This was terrifying news. Each of us wanted to be that One, but not one of us wanted another to fail in favor of our own sobriety.

Joe went on. "Nobody in here or out there can keep you sober. Only your Higher Power can, so you best stay connected to him. And you do it just like you've done in here. You talk to God in the morning. You know, ask Him, 'Help me live in your will, stay sober' and again at night, where you say, 'Thanks for keeping me sober' and all that. Basically, *say please and thank-you, people! He's saved your lives!*" We nodded in humble agreement. "And you make some meetings. They won't keep you sober, but you'll

190

stay connected to your Program and to other drunks and addicts."
Joe crossed his arms and lowered his head as he paced. Then
looking up at each one of us and at all of us, he continued.

"And that leads me to this. The most powerful thing you
can do for your own continued sobriety is helping another
alcoholic or addict. And you'll do it because someone – some old
recovering drunk or addict – did it for you. And outside your
Program? Be of service to others every day. *Be kind to God's kids,
that's what we're talking about here, people!"* he shouted.

Then Joe's loud words snapped from the air, and thick
silence filled the space. I looked up from my wringing hands as Joe
swallowed hard. "Just be kind," he said quietly. "That's what He
really wants. He wants to be with you, and He wants you to be
kind to his other kids."

So Sunday school simple, it's easily forgotten. But
forgetting is a luxury people like us cannot afford. If I forget, I'll
drink. And if I drink, I'll die.

Epilogue

Alcoholics and addicts have a hole in their souls, and we dump our DOC in it to relieve the emptiness and quiet the mind until it stops working and we are truly alone, isolated from God and our fellow man. Then our heads run with self-centered thoughts, so we drink and use some more. But when someone shows us how to quiet the noise in our heads -- not with booze or drugs, but with the clear-headed silence that allows God in—then we can quietly move towards Him, and the closer we get, the better we can hear Him. "Watch over my kids," He urges, and when we do for others, we find the serenity we've always sought. Our lives have direction, meaning and purpose, and we have peace in our formerly traffic-jammed heads and our once broken and hardened hearts. We are no longer alone.

Everyone doesn't make it in sobriety. Wish Joe had been wrong about that. Of the twenty or so from my summer group who stayed in contact, I know of five who have gone out and come back in several times. Eight went out and haven't returned. Four were dead within the first two years. When this harsh reality brings a rush of sadness and heartbreak, I am reminded that to drink and use is our natural state; for us to stay clean and sober is the anomaly. Then I am overcome by a wave of amazement and gratitude that I am sober today.

.

Made in the USA
Charleston, SC
11 June 2016